PRAISE FOR
GIVE YOUR KIDS THE KEYS

Adam and Karie have given to parents many wonderful biblical insights, metaphors and tools for raising children who are influencers in this world. This is a practical handbook for deciphering this vital commission for your own family. Our children are the hope of the future. If they are to be properly equipped, we must learn the parental art of "giving them the keys."

Mark Foreman
Pastor of North Coast Calvary Chapel, Carlsbad, California
Author of *Wholly Jesus: His Surprising Approach to Wholeness and Why It Matters Today*

I would have gladly entrusted my teenaged children to Adam Stadtmiller's care! Adam knows kids and how to foster their transformation into followers of Jesus. He is devoted to the Scriptures and a Christian worldview. Best of all, in *Give Your Kids the Keys*, he shows parents how to navigate this scary culture with positive faith and action instead of fear-based retreat.

Todd Hunter
Rector of the Holy Trinity Anglican Church, Costa Mesa, California
Bishop of Churches for the Sake of Others
Author of *Giving Church Another Chance*

There is no more important or effective way to participate in the mission of God for the glory of God than to raise our children to love and honor Christ. Adam and Karie offer us great insights into doing just that.

Britt Merrick
Founder of the Reality Network of Churches
Author of *Big God: What Happens When We Trust Him*

GIVE YOUR KIDS THE KEYS

Navigating Your Child to a
Personal and Sustainable Faith

ADAM STADTMILLER

WITH KARIE STADTMILLER

Regal

From Gospel Light
Ventura, California, U.S.A.

Published by Regal
From Gospel Light
Ventura, California, U.S.A.
www.regalbooks.com
Printed in the U.S.A.

Library of Congress Cataloging-in-Publication Data
Stadtmiller, Adam.
Give your kids the keys / Adam Stadtmiller with Karie Stadtmiller.
p. cm.
ISBN 978-0-8307-5720-6
1. Parenting—Religious aspects—Christianity. 2. Christian education of children.
I. Stadtmiller, Karie. II. Title.
BV4529.S73 2010
248.8'45—dc22
2010043014

1 2 3 4 5 6 7 8 9 10 11 12 13 14 15 / 20 19 18 17 16 15 14 13 12 11 10

Rights for publishing this book outside the U.S.A. or in non-English languages are
administered by Gospel Light Worldwide, an international not-for-profit ministry.
For additional information, please visit www.glww.org, email info@glww.org, or write
to Gospel Light Worldwide, 1957 Eastman Avenue, Ventura, CA 93003, U.S.A.

To order copies of this book and other Regal products in bulk quantities,
please contact us at 1-800-446-7735.

In 1979, a 13-year-old named Chris Conrad invited my brother Albie on a youth group trip to Disneyland. This simple act of friendship evangelism changed our lives forever. This book is dedicated to him.

Contents

Foreword

By Jim Burns, Ph.D.

President of HomeWord

Author of *10 Building Blocks for a Solid Family*, *Faith Conversations for Families*
and *Creating An Intimate Marriage*

Jesus was asked, "Teacher, which is the greatest commandment in the Law?" (Matt. 22:36). His answer gives us insight into not only how we live our lives but also how we impress our faith on our kids: "Love the Lord your God with all your heart and with all your soul and with all your mind. . . . Love your neighbor as yourself" (vv. 37,39).

In *Give Your Kids the Keys*, Adam will teach you how to bring the main priorities of parenting into the life of your family. In a world with many attractive distractions, this book will remind you of what is most important. Too many people parent by circumstance and chance rather than with true God-honoring purpose. The bottom line isn't raising obedient or even financially successful kids, but rather *raising kids to be responsible adults who love God*. This generation of young people and families are being faced with a culture unlike anything we have ever seen before. It will take committed parents who are willing to put first things first in parenting and draw on God's principles to have a breakthrough in the lives of their family. Adam will guide you to a healthy philosophy of parenting by giving you a foundation to work within your daily life.

My wife, Cathy, and I have tried to make sure we were on the same page with our parenting, but we didn't always find it easy. In fact, we didn't find parenting easy. It was rewarding, absolutely, but one of the most challenging aspects of our lives was (and is) trying to raise our children with a deepened faith and a moral compass that points to a biblical worldview. In this book, we found new phrases to help in our journey, and you will too. "Rear-view parenting" and a "gas pedal parent" are just a few of the principles to help you bring about a closer-knit family.

I love how Adam draws on his own experience with practical and inspiring examples that we can all easily relate to within our own families. He knows kids and families. He has worked with them for years, and he is an expert in reaching out to this generation with a hopeful biblical message. He tells us to set the bar high and know that with God's help, we can become a more solid family that, though far from perfect, strive to love God and love each other.

We have a principle at HomeWord that says, "One of the purposes of the Church is to mentor parents, who will then mentor their children, and the legacy of faith will continue from generation to generation." Every parent needs mentors. Through *Give Your Kids the Keys*, Adam and Karie will lead you and mentor you with sound advice.

As you go through this most important calling in your life, don't forget to stay calm and get as emotionally and spiritually healthy as you possibly can. Then watch your kids learn and develop into faithful followers of Christ. After all, it the ultimate goal to help your kids become those responsible adults mentioned above who have developed a Christ-honoring mission and purpose in life while following the Master?

Foreword

By Mark Foreman

Pastor of North Coast Calvary Chapel, Carlsbad, California

Author of *Wholly Jesus: His Surprising Approach to Wholeness and Why It Matters Today*

It's easier to get pregnant than to get a driver's license. Parents have children every day without any consideration of the future. What's the goal or purpose of parenting? Who are we raising and releasing into the world?

Christian parents usually have a protectionist's goal of raising children who will go to heaven and, along the way, won't smoke, drink or have premarital sex. They ride the brakes throughout their child's upbringing, hoping that when they become an adolescent, or finally a young adult, they won't crash. Our highest value too often is simply safety.

But, as Adam and Karie explain, the goal of parenting is really the same as the goal of Christian discipleship. Jesus said, "You are the salt of the earth. . . . You are the light of the world" (Matt. 5:13-14). Salt and light are substances that permeate and invade their environment. So the goal of raising children is that they would penetrate their spheres of influence with the love and truth of Jesus, using the gifts and resources that God has uniquely given to them.

To accomplish this discipleship goal, we must, as Adam and Karie suggest, become "gas-pedal parents" who are on the offense, not the defense. We must be parents who model and give opportunity to what we hope to see in them. We can give them opportunities to be "salt" and "light" at each stage of their development.

Adam and Karie have given parents many wonderful biblical insights, metaphors and tools for raising children who are influencers—not evaders—in this world. This is a practical handbook for deciphering this vital commission for your own family. I applaud their desire to help Christian parents turn from retreat and boldly return to true discipleship of their kids. Our children are the hope of the future. If they are to be properly equipped we must learn the parental art of "giving them the keys."

Acknowledgments

My gratitude to Jesus cannot be expressed in words. Luckily, I will have all of eternity to find a way to say it.

A thank you goes out to Karie and the girls for putting up with me as I worked on this book. Karie, you are a great second set of eyes, and I so respect you. I can't wait to read your fiction novel. You are my greatest joy this side of heaven.

Thanks also to my mother, Virginia, who had the courage to leave a life of alcoholism and believe that God could restore "the years the locusts have eaten" (Joel 2:25). He surely has!

Thanks also to Boppa Larry and Nanna Pat, for providing us with the love and means to create the childhood memories that will last a lifetime.

To all the youth workers at Skyline Wesleyan who poured so deeply into my life. Your fingerprints were there in my darkest moments.

To all my professors at Point Loma Nazarene and Azusa Pacific. Each of these schools has shaped the core of my theology.

To the parents who added their stories to the content of this book (Mike, Cindy, John, Rachelle, Lauren, Steve and Sherry). You are living examples of parents who have given their kids the keys.

To Tic Long and all the peeps that served with Youth Specialties. Your events have shown me what grace looks like.

I also want to thank all the great people at Gospel Light/Regal. You guys are the real deal!

To the entire North Coast Calvary Chapel family. What a church! We love you guys.

A special thanks to Aaron Chang and his photography. Your gifting captured the very essence and spirit of *Give Your Kids the Keys*. Thanks also to Cheyne Dolly, who let me borrow his sweet '62 Ford Falcon van.

Preface

I will give you the keys of the kingdom of heaven; whatever you bind on earth will be bound in heaven, and whatever you loose on earth will be loosed in heaven.

MATTHEW 16:19

I love the image that Aaron captured for the cover of this book. Who in their right mind would give a set of keys to a three-year old, much less put them in the driver's seat of a classic 1962 Ford Falcon?

I suppose the same question could be asked of Jesus. Are we really to believe that Christ was going to give His disciples the keys to the kingdom of heaven itself? Jesus must have been using hyperbole or some sort of poetic imagery. There was just no way that Jesus was going to give that kind of responsibility and power to that ragtag group of disciples.

Yet while it might seem radical, that is exactly what Jesus did. He did this because He knew something about the release of heavenly kingdoms. Jesus knew that if the kingdom of God were to meet earth, it would have to happen through the hands, feet and lives of those who called Him Lord. God had chosen to unlock the kingdom in partnership. He had chosen to bring the kingdom through His followers.

Nowhere in God's Word have I found an age requirement for loosing the kingdom of heaven. The Bible makes it clear that the keys to the kingdom of God are given to anyone who believes on Jesus as Lord. This includes our kids.

Unfortunately, few kids are raised to understand who they are in Christ or the power they possess in Him. Rarely are children encouraged to bring the kingdom of God on earth. Seldom are they encouraged to walk in their God-given spiritual gifts. Instead, many have been told, "Jesus died on the cross and is coming back again. Now, go out and share your toys and be good boys and girls."

Moralism has become a watered-down version of the gospel. Let me assure you that our children are thirsting for something more. They are yearning to be challenged with a gospel that they can feel and experience to their core.

I pray that this book will help you as a parent to raise world-changers. If you have let status-quo faith pass as exceptional for your family, today is the day to renew your spiritual parenting goals. God believes in your kids. He desires to show them who He is.

As a parent, you have been given the great opportunity to help shape these amazing jars of clay into powerful disciples of the Lord Jesus Himself. May God grant you the power and ability to do this through His grace.

In much love,
Adam, Karie, Lily and Lucy

Go to **www.giveyourkidsthekeys.com** to download small-group discussion guides, watch chapter video introductions, and discuss the concepts of this book.

PART 1

Gas-pedal Parents:

Parenting Toward Engagement and Away from Fear

Fear
by Lily Stadtmiller

I am going to tell you about a time I had fear. On July 9, 2010, I went to Knott's Berry Farm. My dad said I could bring my friend. I chose my friend Trysten. I was having a great time at Knotts. Then my dad and Trysten wanted to go on Montezuma's Revenge!

When we were in line, I was really scared. I wanted to get out of line, but I faced my fears. After the ride was over, I felt my fear go away from me. I noticed that it was really fun. If you do not try to do new things, you won't know what they are like. So try new things.

Gas-pedal Parents

The best defense is a good offense.
CARL VON CLAUSEWITZ

"Oh no, oh no!" were the words I heard, along with a scream, as I woke up out of a dead sleep. I opened my eyes to find us heading toward a massive semi-trailer truck at 65 mph. It was the last day of our yearly snowboard pilgrimage to Mammoth Mountain, in California. My wife, Karie, was driving, and we were headed home. We were about 20 minutes outside of Bishop, and just a few miles from the spot where you can often see herds of elk.

If you have ever been to Mammoth, then you know it rests in the Eastern Sierras. It is one of the most beautiful and majestic places on earth. Just ask John Muir. To get to Mammoth, you need to drive U.S. Route 395. Whether coming in from Reno or Los Angeles, you are in for a Psalm 19 drive. This place "declares the glory of God" and is our family's favorite stretch of road in the universe. It's God's country.

If you have driven the old 395 yourself, then you know that it is one of the most dangerous stretches of road in the great state of California. The lanes are thin, the winds are often high and oncoming traffic is head-on. Driving the 395 is not for rookies.

Startled by my wife's scream, I awoke as my heart raced from a virtual 0 to 60. In front of us loomed a Mack truck. There was nothing I could do. In that moment, Karie had to make a decision that our family's lives depended on. She had three options. She could swerve off the road and into the California high desert, risking loss of control and a possible rollover; she could slam on the brakes and hope to weave back in behind the truck to our right, praying that he would not also brake; or she could hit the gas . . .

Today's parenting is a lot like driving on U.S. Highway 395. Your family is on an amazing journey. It is a long journey that will not only see the lowest lows like Death Valley (see Ps. 23:4), but also the majesty of Mount Whitney, the highest peak in the contiguous United States (see Ps. 18:33).

Navigating the road of parenting is not for the faint of heart. Each bend and turn balances beauty and danger. There are driving snows, steep grades and icy roads. As a mother or father, you are called to navigate this highway called life. It is your job to get your kids safely from point A to point B, eventually giving them the keys to drive life's journey on their own.

That day on 395, Karie decided to use the gas pedal. With our hearts in our throats, Lily, Lucy and I held on as Karie accelerated and swerved back into our lane, narrowly avoiding the bumper of the steel machine heading toward us.

In the moments right after this near tragedy, I had a thought. With my hands still tingling from a rush of blood, awareness came to my head. It was one of those God understandings where our heavenly Father takes a happening and teaches a truth.

This is a paraphrase of what God spoke to my heart in those moments: *Sometimes the best defensive driving tool is the gas pedal. I want you to be gas-pedal parents, and your children gas-pedal kids. I want you to focus on engagement more than disengagement.*

It was a big thought, one that God has been unpacking for me over the months that have followed. What I feel God is telling us is to not parent in fear—to not be parents whose primary purpose is to keep our kids in a bunker or circle the wagons in a defensive position.

I felt He was also saying that He wanted us to make sure that our kids would spend lots of time behind the wheel. He wanted me to understand their God-given spiritual abilities and allow them the opportunity to walk in them, to drive in them. He is calling Karie and me to ride shotgun more often than we chauffeur. He wants us to let our kids learn to know Him as opposed to know about Him.

Gas Pedal vs. Brake Pedal

Like driving, parenting is a delicate balance of acceleration and speed reduction. Notice that I did not use the word "brake." This is because 95 percent of all driving is done without using the brake. Yet, as parents, much of the parenting advice we find in the eBook stores and hear from the pulpits in our churches is often about brake-pedal parenting.

Brake-pedal parenting is parenting by defense. Brake-pedal parenting is based in fear. It is the fear that your kid will hear or experience something that will rob him or her of innocence. Brake-pedal parenting is more about protection than engagement. It's a parenting style that keeps your kids in the backseat as you drive them around life like a tour guide. It is a parent-child model that rarely lets children get behind the wheel to experience the thrill of driving for themselves.

The problem with brake-pedal parenting is that often a kid's first opportunity to take the old spiritual Buick out for a spin comes when he or she is 18. This is what happened to me.

After my dad died when I was 16, my mother stood on the brakes. She followed me to school some days, put me under "house arrest" and even called the cops a few times. Hey, I get it, I am not sure that I would have done any better if I were in her shoes.

The problem with Mom's little plan was that on my eighteenth birthday, I got a letter in the mail from Social Security. It seems that our government has this cool little system where if a dad accrues Social Security and dies before he uses it, then his child gets a handsome little check in the mail.

Thus, on my eighteenth birthday, I went out to the mail and found a check with my name on it for $18,000 and some change.

Literally, within 30 minutes, I left home forever, without saying good-bye, and headed to Palm Springs for one of the craziest weekends of my life.

Within 18 months of that weekend, I was lying in a dark apartment in La Jolla, California, suffering from congestive heart failure caused from a massive crystal meth overdose and crying out to God to save me. Thank God for His great mercy!

So what went wrong? How did a youth-group kid, with heaps of potential, end up almost dead? I knew about the Scriptures; I had gone to camp and rededicated my life so many times that the knees of my jeans had holes worn in them. Deep down, I really loved Jesus.

As I look back, I can see that there were lots of things that led to that dark night. Still, I think I have nailed it down to a couple of key components. First, my Christian upbringing was a lot about what not to do as opposed to what to do. It was more about knowing who not to be than knowing who I truly was in Christ Jesus.[1]

In essence, it was more about the brake pedal than the gas pedal. It was about keeping me safe. It was about knowing the dangers of rock 'n' roll, alcohol and girls, and staying well away. It was about knowledge of what was wrong more than an experience of what was right.

I first came in contact with what I call "gas-pedal parenting" when I was a student at Point Loma Nazarene University in San Diego, California. Tony Campolo was making his yearly college-speaking tour and inviting us all to come spend a summer with him in Philadelphia.

Many people have been critical of Tony over the years. Much of it has to do with his radical approach to Christianity. He was the Francis Chan (author of *Crazy Love*) of my generation, a man who challenged believers to live radically.

That day, Tony made a statement that would change my parenting style forever, even though I was more than 10 years away from becoming a dad. Heck, I didn't even have a wife. Still, I made a decision that day in regard to the kind of parent I wanted to be. Thankfully, I married a woman who would feel the same way.

Tony spoke about raising Christian children. His point was that Christian parenting is more about engagement with proper discipleship than disengagement and protection. He talked about families who had decided to live and work together in the inner city. These families left the comfort of suburbia and private schooling and sent their children to some of the most challenged schools in the nation.

The statement that burned a hole in my soul that day was, "What hope do our public schools have if we take all of the best parents and all of the best students and remove them from the system?" This statement is one of many reasons why our daughter Lily goes to public school today.

This is just one of many decisions that Karie and I have made to allow our kids to be in the world but not of the world. The key is that we are dedicated to being a part of each element of the life we allow them to experience. We are committed to hands-on discipleship. This is why we are on campus every week. Karie is part of the science garden program, and I am a playground dad.

Note that I am not saying to turn your kids over to the wolves without your involvement. Karie and I know many of the teachers and, more importantly, the kids at Lily's school. We are trying to be a light in a sometimes dim place, and we are doing our best to train our girls to have a heart for those who might not know God—while guiding them through the *Twilight* books and movies phenomenon, sometimes salty language and all the other "amazing discipleship opportunities" our little public school has to offer in the way of challenging our girls to live for Jesus when the culture is going the other way. Although I know it sounds counter-Christian-culture, I believe that the best place to teach a child to live out his or her faith is not in the confines of the Christian bubble but rather in the rough and tumble of the world.

Perhaps this quote from John A. Shedd sums it up best: "A ship in harbor is safe—but that is not what ships are built for."[2] I pray that as the parents of the next generation, we will teach our children to sail!

The Darker It Gets, the Harder
We Ride the Brakes

Many parents these days feel that the world is darker than it has ever been. A study of early Rome might change their minds on this, but that is a discussion for another book. In response, some parents employ the brake pedal with more force. The darker the world gets, the harder they stand on the brakes.

Whether or not you decide to homeschool your kids or send them to private or public school is not the point. Rather, the importance rests on the basis of that decision. Are you, as a parent, making faith-filled decisions that can foresee God's faithfulness and promise in all of these possibilities, or are you walking in fear?

For God did not give us a spirit of timidity, but a spirit of power, of love and of self-discipline (2 Tim. 1:7).

The idea of Christians being in the world but not of it, as a part of the Kingdom solution, is basic Christian doctrine. Followers of Jesus are called to be salt in a spiritually tasteless world. Gas-pedal parents know this. They know that children who are kept sequestered from the world, without the ability to process what they see with the help of parents who are committed to disciple them through it, have little hope of immediately being able to do so upon the magic age of 18. Still, many parents raise their kids in this manner. So many parents I meet are gripped in the bondage of fear.

Let me give you an example of the opposite way of parenting. A couple of years ago, our good friends Mike and Cindy decided they were not seeing God clearly enough in their lives. They knew that their kids heard about Jesus on the weekends at church, but they wanted more opportunities to find Him. They wanted opportunities for their kids to be the hands and feet of the Savior. So, as a family, they went looking for God. They went boldly and with an expectation that they would find Him.

Mike and Cindy had a feeling that God might be dwelling in the slums of Tijuana, just south of the U.S./Mexico border, close to where we live. People with better judgment told them this was not a safe adventure to take kids on. The roads were dangerous, the violence in Mexican border towns was increasing and diseases were prevalent.

Any "wise" parent would know that trips like this were for older kids, not young children. The thing is that Mike and Cindy are gas-pedal parents. They knew that the spiritual values their kids would learn on this trip were eternal and outweighed those risks. They also had faith in the God whom they felt called their family to the sewers and slums of Mexico, knowing that in the end, their lives were in His protective hands (see Ps. 5:11). They were also committed to being there every step of the way.

From that point on, about four Saturdays per year, Mike, Cindy, Ashlyn (7) and Lauren (5) would wake up at 4:30 A.M. and head off to the cold, dark parking lot outside of our church. With coffee and greasy donuts in hand, they would journey south an hour and a half until they came to one of the poorer areas of the world to spend the day building homes for the poor with Baja Christian Ministries.[3]

Every Sunday after one of their trips I would hear the stories of how God had shown up. How a flat tire had led to an opportunity to share their faith or how they did not have money to build the home just days before, but after praying, the exact amount would come in the mail. Over and over again, God showed up and they recognized Him in their midst. Over and over again, Ashlyn and Lauren went from being kids who knew about God to kids who actively knew Him!

It's Not Just About Fear

The second component I learned that day on Highway 395 is that gas-pedal parenting is not just about parenting away from fear. That's only one aspect of it. It is also about awareness, empowerment and engagement. It is about letting God loose in all areas of your life so that your children might come to know Jesus in a real way. It is about finding the areas of your life that are in cruise control and switching back over to manual drive. Better yet, it is about letting your kids have the keys to their spiritual life while you navigate awhile and ride shotgun. We'll look at this aspect in the next few chapters.

Getting There

Our culture is overrun with fear. If you don't believe me, just watch the nightly news. Fear is the predominant message—every adjective purposely placed to drive the emotions. This preoccupation with fear is one of the reasons for the dramatic increase in anxiety disorder among adults and children.[4]

The Scriptures are clear that we are never to make decisions out of fear. Fear is a lack of understanding of God's truth, for in God there is no fear. Decisions based in fear will not bear the same healthy fruit as decisions based upon faith in God. This is true no matter what the circumstances surrounding a decision.

Here is a list of questions to help you think through the motives behind the way you parent your children.

- Am I more worried or faith-filled when it comes to my child's future?

- Do I more often think about what to keep my child from than about what to involve him in?

- Even though my child has the maturity to attend an overnight camp or sleep over, do I usually keep her home because of my fear?

- Do I regularly warn my children of the dangers of the world more than the truth of God's protection?

- Am I more fearful of the influence of the Web and other media than I am trusting in God's Word to shape my child?

- Do I have full faith in God's ability to protect my children, no matter where they are?[5]

- What is the prevailing tone of your conversations? Keep a journal this week of the conversations that surround your life. What did you talk about? What did you say? What did your kids say? What did other people you interacted with say? What did you hear on TV and continue to think about?

In the coming week, write down each time you hear a statement based in fear. Take each of these statements and compare them to the Word of God. Since fear is based in a lie, try to determine the lie behind each of these statements. Here is an example I recently dealt with:

The Statement: "Wow, what a beautiful daughter you have. I'll pray for you when she becomes a teenager!"

The Lie: "Since your daughter is attractive, she will have a proclivity to sin and/or a difficult teen experience." (While I know that statements like this can be easily discarded to the "I was only joking" category, I still find them extremely powerful in creating a mindset of fear versus a mind of Christ.)

The Word: If your kids know the Word and hide it in their hearts, they will have the fuel to sustain them through any season of life.

> Do not let them [God's words] depart from your sight; keep them in the midst of your heart (Prov. 4:21, NASB).

> Now then, my sons, listen to me and do not depart from the words of my mouth (Prov. 5:7, NASB).

> The highway of the upright is to depart from evil; he who watches his way preserves his life (Prov. 16:17, NASB).

The Truth: God has the ability to sustain children through the teenage years. It is His will and desire to keep teenagers

walking in His truth and His will. God has not relin-
quished these years to the devil. I wish the same could be
said for many parents who accept that disobedience or a
loss of communication and friendship with their child is
a necessary result of being a teenager.

By doing the above exercise, you will begin to help your family
grow deep roots into the soil of God's truth, and also weed out the
fear. The conversations of your life will increasingly line up with
the truth of God's Word, and the decisions you make will bear the
marks and the fruit of deep faith as opposed to fear. Imagine the
possibilities!

Notes

1. Both my junior high and senior high experiences at Skyline Wesleyan Church in San
   Diego, California, were an exception to this in many ways. Those ministries were en-
   gagement-oriented.

2 John A. Shedd, *Salt from My Attic* (Portland, ME: The Mosher Press, 1928).

3. See www.bajachristian.org.

4. "The Numbers Count: Mental Disorders in America," National Institute of Mental
   Health. http://www.nimh.nih.gov/health/publications/the-numbers-count-mental-
   disorders-in-america.shtml#Anxiety.

5. Of course, in making this statement, I am not suggesting that as a parent you not be
   vigilant in wisdom. Allow the Holy Spirit to guide you.

CHAPTER 2

Shepherds in the Wilderness

Many of us crucify ourselves between two thieves—
regret for the past and fear of the future.

FULTON OURSLER

Several years ago, I was a contestant on *Hollywood Squares*. It was "Survivor Week," and most of the people in the squares were members of the cast of the "Africa season" of *Survivor*.

About halfway through the show, I landed on the secret square. If you are not familiar with the rules of the game, correctly answering the secret square question can win you a really cool prize. The square in question was worth a seven-day Caribbean adventure aboard an old-school ocean schooner. Thanks to some help from Brad Paisley, I won the trip.[1]

As soon as we got home from Hollywood, Karie and I began an excited search of the Web to discover what we could about the adventure that awaited us. Don't you love researching for a trip? It is so easy to picture yourself and your family experiencing the amazing sights, smells and tastes the destination has to offer.

Whenever we go on vacation, we are also aware of the possible dangers. In a couple of weeks, we will go to Yosemite with our girls. We will have to put our food and toiletries in bear boxes. Also, Lucy can't swim yet; and since our campsite is not far from a swift-moving stream, we will need to keep our eyes on her. While bears and swift-moving water are real concerns to be aware of, they do not dominate our thoughts. These realities won't keep us from going on the camping trip. They won't keep us away from all the goodness and promise this trip has to offer.

Taking Possession

During the first few years of Lily's life, I did not live this way. Rather than seeing Lily's future as a land of God's blessing and promise for her to possess, I feared the day she would pack up and move out. I was terrified of middle school and high school; and don't even get me started about college! In the same way that you would frantically rush around and gather your most precious belongings before an approaching flood, I prepared for Lily's departure as if a disaster was on its way. I was scared to death.

As God's truth began to wash away the fear, I landed on a new and exciting perspective. It has changed the way we parent to the core. We now see that Lily and Lucy's future is full of God's goodness. There are giants in the land, but as a parent, I don't want to be counted as one of the spies who return from the land of promise with a bad report.

When you begin to see your children's transition into new territories as an opportunity for them to possess the promises of God, you start parenting in the spirit of strength and courage that Joshua walked in as he led the children of Israel into their inheritance.

The Future Promised Land

Part of the inheritance you are leaving your children is their future. We often see inheritance in monetary form, something that will make life a little easier. I would argue that teaching your children how to grasp the land of their future in Christ is more valuable than any gift you can leave them in the physical realm.

This was the specific calling on Joshua's life:

After the death of Moses the servant of the LORD, the LORD said to Joshua son of Nun, Moses' aide: "Moses my servant is dead. Now then, you and all these people, get ready to cross the Jordan River into the land I am about to give to them—to the Israelites. I will give you every place where you set your foot, as I promised Moses. Your territory will extend from the desert to Lebanon, and from the great river, the Euphrates—all the Hittite country—to the Great Sea on the west. No one will be able to stand up against you all the days of your life. As I was with Moses, so I will be with you; I will never leave you nor forsake you.

"Be strong and courageous, because you will lead these people to inherit the land I swore to their forefathers to give them. Be strong and very courageous. Be careful to obey all the law my servant Moses gave you; do not turn from it to the right or to the left, that you may be successful wherever you go. Do not let this Book of the Law depart from your mouth; meditate on it day and night, so that you may be careful to do everything written in it. Then you will be prosperous and successful. Have I not commanded you? Be strong and courageous. Do not be terrified; do not be discouraged, for the LORD your God will be with you wherever you go."

So Joshua ordered the officers of the people: "Go through the camp and tell the people, 'Get your supplies ready. Three days from now you will cross the Jordan here to go in and take possession of the land the LORD your God is giving you for your own'" (Josh. 1:1-11).

Like Joshua, you have a calling to lead your children into the promised lands of the upper school years and beyond. Just as God called the Israelites to walk in faith into a new territory, you, too, are called and have been given the gifts, weapons and commands that will enable you to consume its riches and blessings.

The devil wants you to look at the land on your horizon in the same way the unfaithful spies looked upon the country of God from the book of Numbers. He wants you to cower. He wants you to back away in fear. He wants you to spend more time in worry than in faith.

This type of approach and perspective is what caused the children of the spies of Israel to spend 40 years wandering in the wilderness as shepherds instead of living off the fat of the Promised Land. Numbers 13 gives the account of these gas-pedal parents.

God's Call to Survey the Land

"The LORD said to Moses, 'Send some men to explore the land of Canaan, which I am giving to the Israelites. From each ancestral tribe send one of its leaders'" (Num. 13:1-2). Moses chose to send leaders to spy out the land. He knew that the perspective of the leaders was what, in the end, would give the people the fortitude they needed when things got difficult to possess the land they had been given.

Moses' Call to Survey the Obstacles and Report on the Goodness of the Land

"When Moses sent them to explore Canaan, he said, 'Go up through the Negev and on into the hill country. See what the land is like and whether the people who live there are strong or weak, few or many. What kind of land do they live in? Is it good or bad? What kind of towns do they live in? Are they unwalled or fortified? How is the soil? Is it fertile or poor? Are there trees on it or not? Do your best to bring back some of the fruit of the land' (It was the season for the first ripe grapes.)" (Num. 13:17-20).

Moses was not glib in his approach to accessing blessings and dangers. He was diligent in his stewardship of discovery. When he did take the land, he was going to be prepared. You can be sure that when Moses sent out the spies, it was not to decide if they should take the land or not, but rather the manner in which they would possess it. Can you see the parenting parallels?

The Report of the Unfaithful Spies

"At the end of forty days they returned from exploring the land. They came back to Moses and Aaron and the whole Israelite community at Kadesh in the Desert of Paran. There they reported to them and to the whole assembly and showed them the fruit of the land. They gave Moses this account: 'We went into the land to which you sent us, and it does flow with milk and honey! Here is its fruit. But the people who live there are powerful, and the cities are fortified and very large. We even saw descendants of Anak there. The Amalekites live in the Negev; the Hittites, Jebusites and Amorites live in the hill country; and the Canaanites live near the sea and along the Jordan'" (Num. 13:25-29).

The report of the unfaithful spies came back with the assessment of abundance, but it was mired in fear. *There was no heart to possess the land.* I would go so far as to say that if you, as a parent, have a similar view of your child's future, then you will run the same risk.

Parents who enter these phases of life without the perspective of faith often lose heart in these times. They revert to tactics rather than godly, faith-filled parenting. They stand on the brakes, forgetting that it is one of the most dangerous things you can do when driving downhill. I don't blame them. Fear causes a desire to slam on the brakes when a gentle clutch and downshift might be all that is required.

The Report of Caleb and Joshua

"Then Caleb silenced the people before Moses and said, 'We should go up and take possession of the land, for we can certainly do it'" (Num. 13:30).

Caleb displayed a godly confidence and an eagerness to possess the land. "We can certainly do it!" was his assessment. When you are spying out the land of your child's future, the tough question for you as a parent is, "Do you feel godly confidence and an eagerness to help them possess it?"

The Result of the Unfaithful Report as Spoken by God

"Your children, however, whom you said would become a prey— I will bring them in, and they will know the land which you have rejected. But as for you, your corpses will fall in this wilderness. Your sons shall be shepherds for forty years in the wilderness, and they will suffer for your unfaithfulness, until your corpses lie in the wilderness. According to the number of days which you spied out the land, forty days, for every day you shall bear your guilt a year, even forty years, and you will know My opposition. I, the LORD, have spoken, surely this I will do to all this evil congregation who are gathered together against Me. In this wilderness they shall be destroyed, and there they will die" (Num. 14:31-35, *NASB*).

Give thanks that we are not living in Old Testament times. Jesus' death on the cross and His blood shed for our sins has opened to us a grace that was unknown in the time of Joshua the son of Nun. Today if we fail in our faith, it is not with the same result these people suffered. Romans 8 assures us of that. Thanks be to our great God!

But there is still a powerful lesson for us here. The future of the literal children of Israel was profoundly altered due to their parents' faith, perspective and understanding, and they suffered because of it. Instead of seeing the land set before them as a land to be possessed, they saw it as one where they would be destroyed. Instead of believing in the Word of God for their future, they looked to the world for their destiny.

Their children did not get to spend their teens, twenties and thirties possessing a rich land full of milk, honey and fat grapes; they were left to be "shepherds in the wilderness."

Is it possible that the epidemic losses (60 percent) of Christian teens into their twenties abandoning the Church has something to do with the perspective we are raising them in?[2] I believe it is part of the equation. A study by The Barna Group shows the following:

> Despite strong levels of spiritual activity during the teen years, most twentysomethings disengage from active participation in the Christian faith during their young adult years—and often beyond that. *In total, six out of ten twentysomethings were involved in a church during their teen years, but have failed to translate that into active spirituality during their*

early adulthood. . . . Much of the ministry to teenagers in America needs an overhaul—not because churches fail to attract significant numbers of young people, but because so much of those efforts are not creating a sustainable faith beyond high school. There are certainly effective youth ministries across the country, but the levels of disengagement among twentysomethings suggest that youth ministry fails too often at discipleship and faith formation. A new standard for viable youth ministry should be—not the number of attendees, the sophistication of the events or the "cool" factor of the youth group—but whether teens have the commitment, passion and resources to pursue Christ intentionally and wholeheartedly after they leave the youth ministry nest.[3]

While I agree with this study, I would assert that church ministry is not the total solution. The study needs to be taken back a step further in time and applied to the home. While youth and college ministries are a place to finely sand a faith that has already been carved, they aren't always a good place for hewing it from raw stone.

"Shepherding" in the Wilderness

Looking back, I fully understand what being a shepherd in the wilderness is like. I cannot tell you how many times I shared the gospel while under the influence of alcohol or some narcotic. I distinctly remember doing drugs with a friend and telling him that Jesus was Lord. I told him how I did not really want to be doing this and would soon be returning back to God. If I did this once, I did it 50 times. I was a shepherd in the wilderness.

I don't want to make the complete jump to saying that if a child has wandering years it is because of a parent's perspective and understanding. I feel that this is a bit too guilt-producing. In the end, your children do have a free will. Even Adam and Eve turned away, and they were fathered/created by God Himself.

Still, as I look back, I can see in my case that I was never prepared to possess the lands that lay before me. As I mentioned earlier, I was told of all the giants the world had to offer, rather than seeing my future as an opportunity to claim everywhere I set my foot and possess the land.

I will give you every place where you set your foot, as I promised Moses (Josh. 1:3).

Let me assure you that God is not dreading your child's teens and twenties. He has filled those years full of promise! If you have lived in fear of these years, I challenge you to get your perspective in line with biblical truth. *Remember that what you believe as truth finds its expression in the life you create by your decisions. Understanding guides decisions.*

Since coming to this realization, we have done our best to parent away from fear. Decisions based in faith and promise result in a life of faith and promise. Decisions based in fear create fear.

I cannot tell you how much freedom Karie and I have experienced since taking on the perspective of the good spies. Now when we talk about the future with our girls, we speak with hope.

One way we do this is by taking our girls on spying journeys. For instance, last night, when the girls and I were watching a movie about a loving grandfather and his granddaughter, I felt God give me a picture of what being a grandparent would look like. I got excited. I paused the movie and said to my girls, "I can't wait to meet my grandkids!" I started telling them about all the great things I was going to do with them and what great moms they were going to be. I talked about the great husbands they were going to marry who would become great dads, and how much fun it was going to be to be their kids' grandpa.

By having conversations like this, I feel that we are letting the girls survey the goodness of the land before them. Even though my girls did not really want to look that far into the future ("Yucky"), I wanted to let them see the blessings. I wanted them to taste the grapes of the land. I wanted to speak a good report of faith in front of them. I wanted them to know that I believe in them to make right decisions that will guide them to this future. Knowing where you are going makes it a lot easier to know how to get there.

The Place of Health and Wealth

Just to be clear, I am not proclaiming a prosperity gospel. The Word of God is clear that the life in Christ is more about the cross than it is about finding and having everything you want. Just because you believe something does not mean that you will get it. I struggle greatly with a gospel that promises anything more than salvation and knowing Jesus Christ crucified, risen and coming again.

> These things that I once considered valuable, I now consider worthless for Christ. It's far more than that! I consider everything else worthless because I'm much better off knowing Christ Jesus my Lord. It's because of him that I think of everything as worthless. I threw it all away in order to gain Christ and to have a relationship with him. This means that I didn't receive God's approval by obeying his laws. The opposite is true! I have God's approval through faith in Christ. This is the approval that comes from God and is based on faith that knows Christ. Faith knows the power that his coming back to life gives and what it means to share his suffering. In this way I'm becoming like him in his death, with the confidence that I'll come back to life from the dead (Phil. 3:7-11, *GOD'S WORD*).

The inheritance I am espousing is about knowing Christ and His eternal riches. It is about believing that your children can be sustained in Jesus throughout these seasons and in these lands. My main contention is that I often see parents believing a reverse prosperity gospel. They believe in the bad that might beset them. I do believe that this can become a self-fulfilling prophecy. There is no sin in reflecting a picture of God's goodness and hope to your children. The caveat is that you disciple them to love and follow Jesus no matter what life throws at them.

Giant-killing Faith

When it comes time to tell our girls about the giants in the land, we will. When we do, we pray it will be with the faith of Joshua, who when preparing to finally take the land said this:

> They said to Joshua, "The LORD has surely given the whole land into our hands; all the people are melting in fear because of us" (Josh. 2:24).

> Joshua told the people, "Consecrate yourselves, for tomorrow the LORD will do amazing things among you" (Josh. 3:5).

> Our great hope is to create a giant-killing faith and expectation within our children. This is not too high a goal. Scripture gives us a great human example of a giant killed by a boy named David. When everyone else cowered in fear, David struck down the largest giant of his day.

> So David triumphed over the Philistine with a sling and a stone; without a sword in his hand he struck down the Philistine and killed him. David ran and stood over him. He took hold of the Philistine's sword and drew it from the scabbard. After he killed him, he cut off his head with the sword (1 Sam. 17:50-51).

Getting There

In the journal you started last chapter, write down all of the lands that your child can possess. Examples of this could be sports teams, high school, the teenage years, education, marriage, and so on. Next, write down all of the fears associated with those lands.

Finally, write down what you feel those lands would look like if your children were able to possess them in the fullness of faith and God's blessing. In other words, what does a middle-school experience look like where God pours out His blessing on your child?

Pray often, asking God for His vision for your child's future. Too often as believers we apply our worldly perspective to a person's destiny. The only way to truly parent your child into their destiny is with a true revelation from God. Trust the Holy Spirit to guide you into this. When you feel that you get an insight, write it down and begin to test it.

Finally, take your children on spying journeys. If you have a preschooler, take your child to his or her new kindergarten class before the year begins. Let your child play on the play equipment. Look at the names of all the kids who will be in your child's class. Talk about what great friends your child is going to have. Tell your child how much fun it is going to be to learn. Tell him or her that God has great things in store for his or her future! Tell them that when they get there Jesus will be waiting for them.

Notes

1. If you want to see me on the show, you can go to my website adamstadtmiller.com. It is there in all its lack of glory.

2. "Most Twenty-somethings Put Christianity on the Shelf Following Spiritually Active Teen Years," the Barna Group, September 11, 2006. http://www.barna.org/teens-next-gen-articles/147-most-twentysomethings-put-christianity-on-the-shelf-following-spir-itually-active-teen-years.

3. Ibid., emphasis added.

CHAPTER 3

High Mountains and Deep Water

You've climbed the highest mountain in the world.
What's left? It's all downhill from there. You've got to set your
sights on something higher than Everest.
WILLI UNSOELD[1]

Highway 38 is the back way to Big Bear, California—a small, often snow-covered resort mountain town just outside of Los Angeles. Highway 38 is the way we always travel when we are heading up to Karie's parents' cabin for a family getaway. We love this drive and often feel that its beauty stands in contrast with much of what you think Southern California has to offer in regard to scenery. It really does have a Colorado feel to it, especially when the skies are blue after a fresh snow.

One of the sights we love on the 38 is Mount San Gorgonio. Gorgonio is the highest point in Southern California, and stands chiseled in gray granite above the tree line at 11,503 feet.[2] Climbing Gorgonio is a great ambition and one that, while not easy, can be accomplished by any well-conditioned individual in a day, starting from the Fish Creek trailhead.

Gorgonio is also one of the seven summits of Big Bear. Okay, they are not "the" seven summits that stand along with Kilimanjaro and Denali, but they are a pretty cool challenge for an eight-year-old and her dad! Lily and I will be starting our push this summer to conquer them all.

To put things in perspective, Mount Whitney, which I mentioned in the first chapter, sits at 14,505 feet. While this is high enough to cause altitude sickness, it is still considered low in regard to the highest peaks of the world. Even Mount Everest's north base camp in Tibet rests at 17,087 feet, and this is just the base camp. It takes another long 11,915 feet to reach the highest place on earth.[3] Yet this feat was achieved in May 2010, when 13-year-old Jordan Romero, from Big Bear, California, became the youngest person to ever summit this giant. Before he was about to make the ascent, he wrote on his blog: "Every step I take is finally toward the biggest goal of my life, to stand on top of the world."[4]

We are living in the age of the kid. For good or bad, kids are doing more than ever before. Whether sailing around the world solo, a feat just accomplished by 16-year-old Jessica Watson (with even younger sailors standing in line behind her), or winning Olympic gold, kids are going big.

As I did research for this chapter, I came across some amazing kids. Most of them had a few things in common. The majority of these inspiring stories were of kids accomplishing something that had been modeled to them all their lives. Jordan's father is an accomplished climber and professional adventure racer. Ever since Jordan's earliest years, he had seen his father live a life that he aspired to and emulated. His father modeled this spirit of adventure in a way that his son could grasp. It did not seem out of his son's reach.

I think this is such a powerful lesson that begs a powerful question: What are you modeling for your child to emulate, and does it encourage your child to be his or her best? If you are a parent whose number-one priority is pleasure or the mighty dollar (or euro these days), then don't be surprised when your nine-year-old's desires follow that pattern.

Another aspect that stood out to me in reading stories of young people's endeavors was the faith their parents had in their abilities. To use the previous chapter's term, these are "gas-pedal parents." How many parents would have looked at that nine-year-old and said something like, "Oh, that's nice, honey; maybe one day I'll take you to a movie about climbing mountains"? Jordan's parents, on the other hand, saw something deeper in their child and said, "Okay, let's start climbing."

While I got really excited and encouraged about all of these stories, there was one thing that began to stand out. All of the examples I came across were stories that highlighted worldly accomplishment—achievements that were not eternal, that would pass away. There were no stories that had headlines reading, "Twelve-year-old becomes youngest to start an orphanage in India" or "Seven-year-old feeds 1,000 homeless on Thanksgiving Day." I'm not saying that these stories are not out there, but I am a pretty good Web search-engine detective, and I couldn't find any.

I wonder why this is so, when we, as Christians, have a God who backs our actions done in Him. Why don't we hear more about believing kids who are making a huge impact in the world? Kids who, with their parents' discipleship, are changing other people's lives in dramatic, eye-catching ways?

I think that one of the reasons we have such a lack of spiritual productivity from Christian kids is that their parents are unintentionally hindering them.

Do I think that Jordan's reaching the top of the world is a great thing? Yes, I do. Do I think it changes the world? Sure it does. He has inspired many to follow their dreams. My point is that I hope many of the dreams that he inspires are ones that call kids to live beyond themselves—to climb a greater summit and build a greater Kingdom.

I think that one of the reasons we have such a lack of spiritual productivity from Christian kids is that their parents are unintentionally hindering them. I think this happens in numerous ways while parents allow staying in "base-camp spirituality" to pass as exceptional.

This definitely happens when Christian parents focus solely on morality rather than true, sold-out experiential faith. The high bar for so many of us as parents is to raise good kids. Good kids know what is right from wrong and live their life according to the rules, but they run the risk of not experiencing the full and dynamic life in Christ to which they are called.

Recently, I was having dinner with Britt Merrick, the author of *Big God* and pastor of Reality Church in Carpinteria, California.[5] Britt said that he thought the idea of moralism is at the core of a lot of our teaching in the area of Christian child spiritual development. His point was that if you look at many of the children's Bibles and curriculum in the market right now, you'll see that instead of teaching the true gospel in all of its intent they focus on teaching kids to be good and to follow a law of sorts. His direct quote, as best I can remember, was, "Hey, kids, Jesus died and suffered on the cross, now share your toys and be good boys and girls."

Parents who engage their children in the spiritual heights are parents who know that the purpose of God's redemptive work in the world is not to teach us to be good. Instead, the purpose of the gospel is to allow us to have an eternally transformational relationship of engagement with a risen Christ. We can never be good (see Rom. 3:12), but God is, and He has called us to live powerfully in Him and His goodness and to be transformed by allowing Him to live through us. In the end, good kids don't often change the world, but kids transformed by the power of the gospel do! As a matter of fact, they change heaven and eternity as well. For this reason, I pray to God that my kids and yours don't end up just being good kids!

How High Are Your Parenting Goals?

I think the next possible obstacle kids need to overcome is their parents' lack of belief and/or interest in their spiritual ability. Unfortunately, this is not true about so many of their kids' other abilities. Most of us do not have a difficult time dreaming of our child hitting the game-winning home run in the World Series, or graduating with honors from one of the best schools in the nation. We are really good at seeing our kids' worldly potential and gearing our parenting toward it.

Hey, I do this myself! Just last week I was at Lucy's two-year-olds ballet class. You can bet I was watching her closely to see if she had any ability in the area of dance. My mind flashed forward to the day when Karie and I would attend her opening as the prima donna of the National English Ballet. Before we even left the parking lot I was dreaming of a personal dance instructor for Lucy so she could get to the next level.

Sports parents are great at this. It's all about getting their kids started as young as possible. You know, those classic pictures of a child in diapers on a surfboard or swinging the old nine-iron as a toddler. The sad thing for this generation of children is that many parents don't have the same enthusiasm when it comes to the Kingdom-building potential their kids are gifted for and called to.

Do you think that most Christian parents are aware of the spiritual gifts their children possess?[6] Do they believe that a three-year-old can be an evangelist? How many parents are looking intently for things like a heart of mercy or a spirit of encouragement within their child instead of just an ability to achieve in the classroom or playing field? Stop me if I am wrong, but I don't see a lot of photos of people's toddlers handing out turkeys to homeless people in the same way I see what makes the email rounds and Facebook photo galleries.

Believing in the world-changing, kingdom-bringing spiritual ability of our children is basic Christian parenting. It's basic because the Word of God is replete with story after story of God using children and young people to transform the world. In the Scriptures we find:

1. **David:** a sixth-grade future king who fights God's battles while slaying lions, bears, giants and, in the end, liberating a nation from oppression.

But David said to Saul, "Your servant has been keeping his father's sheep. When a lion or a bear came and carried off a sheep from the flock, I went after it, struck it and rescued the sheep from its mouth. When it turned on me, I seized it by its hair, struck it and killed it. Your servant has killed both the lion and the bear; this uncircumcised Philistine will be like one of them, because he has defied the armies of the living God. The Lord who delivered me from the paw of the lion and the paw of the bear will deliver me from the hand of this Philistine." Saul said to David, "Go, and the Lord be with you" (1 Sam. 17:34-37).

2. **Timothy:** from infancy, he had the ability to know and be changed by the Scriptures.

From infancy you have known the holy Scriptures, which are able to make you wise for salvation through faith in Christ Jesus (2 Tim. 3:15).[7]

3. **John the Baptist:** an unborn fetus who was able to experience the touch of the Holy Spirit.

When Elizabeth heard Mary's greeting, the baby leaped in her womb, and Elizabeth was filled with the Holy Spirit (Luke 1:41).

4. **Mary:** a middle-schooler who would become the mother of God.

But after he had considered this, an angel of the Lord appeared to him in a dream and said, "Joseph son of David, do not be afraid

to take Mary home as your wife, because what
is conceived in her is from the Holy Spirit"
(Matt. 1:20).

God believes in kids. He believes in your kid(s). He believes in
them so much that when Jesus tells us how to inherit the kingdom of God, He points to them as the model. He believes in them
so much that when they dream about climbing His highest summits He says, "Let's start climbing!"

If you don't believe that your child has the potential or that
God might call them to do something this great, then you need
to wake up and get your understanding of Christian parenting in
line with the truth of God's Word. God has greater aspirations for
your children than just hoping they make it through high school
without having sex. So should you. If you don't, you are running
the risk of just raising good kids.

Finding balance in this parenting pursuit will be one of the
biggest challenges of your life. My old boss, Paul, of Soul Survivor
USA, used to say, "Extremes are easy." I am not proposing that you
become "The Great Santini," a hard-driving father played by actor
Robert Duvall who had such high hopes and aspirations for his
son that he ended up driving him away. Being a gas-pedal parent
does not mean that you drive with the pedal to the spiritual metal.
Instead I am encouraging you to believe in your kids and give them
the opportunity to live spiritually challenging, spiritually dangerous lives—lives lived climbing high in the mountains of faith.

Is this not what happened when Jesus first laid eyes on the disciples? These men would, one day, change the world forever. None
were of particular status or position, having been passed over by
the many rabbis that trolled the countryside looking for the best
and the brightest.

Jesus, seeing with spiritual eyes beyond the confines of a worldly
perspective, saw eternal potential. Where the world saw common
fishermen, Jesus saw world changers. Where the world saw spiritual
infants, Jesus saw the hope of the gospel. For these men, a dynamic
life in Christ started with an invitation into deep water.

One day as Jesus was standing by the Lake of Gennesaret, with the people crowding around him and listening to the word of God, he saw at the water's edge two boats, left there by the fishermen, who were washing their nets. He got into one of the boats, the one belonging to Simon, and asked him to put out a little from shore. Then he sat down and taught the people from the boat.

When he had finished speaking, he said to Simon, "Put out into deep water, and let down the nets for a catch."

Simon answered, "Master, we've worked hard all night and haven't caught anything. But because you say so, I will let down the nets."

When they had done so, they caught such a large number of fish that their nets began to break. So they signaled their partners in the other boat to come and help them, and they came and filled both boats so full that they began to sink.

When Simon Peter saw this, he fell at Jesus' knees and said, "Go away from me, Lord; I am a sinful man!" For he and all his companions were astonished at the catch of fish they had taken, and so were James and John, the sons of Zebedee, Simon's partners.

Then Jesus said to Simon, "Don't be afraid; from now on you will catch men." So they pulled their boats up on shore, left everything and followed him (Luke 5:1-11).

If you have not done this already, it is time to call your kids into the deep water. The story of Jesus and the call of the first disciples will give you a pattern for how to do this. Jesus starts with the Word of God and brings it to them in the everyday surroundings of their life. These were fishermen, and so he talked about the Word of God near the seashore, using analogies from the environment.

You will see, in the coming chapters, your need to saturate the normalcy of the life you live with the Word of God. God's Word is the fuel for a radical life. Your goal is to unshackle God's Word from the confines of a bedtime ritual, weekly Sunday School and a brief prayer before meal times, letting it invade every part of your life.

When He was done speaking to the crowd, Jesus got into the disciples' boat. You can be sure this was not a random act. The Scripture mentions that there were two boats, but Jesus chose to get into the one owned by Simon Peter. In this way, He was singling out this disciple. It was a huge honor to have this revered Rabbi in his boat.

Rabbis in Jesus' time were very particular about whom they associated themselves with. Most would never step into the boat of a common fisherman, but this is what Jesus did.

By doing this, Jesus was saying, "You matter." And you can be confident that the future disciples understood this very unique act and took it as a huge honor.

The problem with Jesus, though, is that if you give Him an inch, He will take an eternity. So, like Jesus does, He challenged them to get their feet wet and push off a little from shore.

Once they were comfortable, Jesus upped the ante. "Put out into deep water, and let down the nets for a catch," He said. What Jesus was actually saying was, "Come with me, let's go to the spiritual deep end."

Before long these disciples were seeing a miracle. Jesus had called them to live beyond the futility of net washing and shallow waters. The result? Remember that other boat in the Luke 5 text? I have a feeling that it was the boat they summoned to help with the overwhelming catch. In other words, by having someone who believed enough in them to call them into the deep waters of spirituality, they themselves gained the ability to do the same.

Deep-water Fishing

This week I was having lunch with my good friend Steve. He and his wife, Sherry, have committed themselves to deep-water parenting. As we ate, Steve talked about how, ever since their kids were little, he and Sherry have done their best to not only let them know about Jesus, but also to experience Him.

A few years back, Sherry had the idea to bless kids who were battling cancer. She gathered the troops (their three kids and a group of third-grade girls from their daughters' school) and headed off to Children's Hospital to give care packages to some of the most seriously ill children in the county. The key was to let her kids do it. Here is an excerpt from Sherry's email to me about this project:

> The project was born out of the idea that our children so often have the thinking that "charity" means that Mom and Dad write a check and send it off somewhere. I wanted the girls in our group (third-graders) to take more owner-ship, make more sacrifice and then have the blessing of see-ing where, and to whom, their efforts benefited. This was a charity project but truly, selfishly for our kids. I wanted the impact to be on our kids . . . not just the recipients.

This one-time experiment led to a regular family experience. For the next couple of years, these children and their families be-came a part of Steve's family's story. In the process their kids ended up in the deep waters of spirituality. They learned how to process real-life events. They learned how to pray for the sick. They learned compassion; and in the end they got a little closer to being spiri-tually dangerous kids, kids who could climb a spiritual Everest and swim in the depths of God.

Spoiler Alert

Employing the biblical principles in this book will ruin your kid's life. The good news is that Jesus came to do just that. C. S. Lewis says it this way:

> Jesus says, "Give me all of you!!! I don't want so much of your time, so much of your talents and money, and so much of your work. I want YOU!!! ALL OF YOU!! I have not come to torment or frustrate the natural man or

woman, but to KILL IT! No half measures will do. I don't want to only prune a branch here and a branch there; rather I want the whole tree out! Hand it over to me, the whole outfit, all of your desires, all of your wants and wishes and dreams. Turn them ALL over to me, give yourself to me and I will make of you a new self—in my image. Give me yourself and in exchange I will give you Myself. My will, shall become your will. My heart, shall become your heart.[8]

If you are hearing me proclaim some kind of radical approach to Christian parenting, then you are mistaken. What I am proposing is basic Christianity. It goes no further and demands no more than the standard set by the Word of God. This is how we are called to live. This is how we are called to parent. It only seems radical when the common standard has fallen to a point that would be unrecognizable to the believers of Jesus' day.

The Jesus Approach to Deep-water Faith

Much of Jesus' care for the disciples can be directly translated to parenting. In Luke 5, we find some key prescriptions for helping our children live that deep-water faith.

1. *While they were fishing:* Jesus made the Word of God centric to the conversation of His life. He took the deep teachings of Scripture and made them relevant to His hearers while they were fishing. He drew upon His surroundings and turned them into powerful metaphors and stories that brought the truth of God's Word to their doorstep. He allowed the Word of God to defy the confines of spiritual places, releasing it into the everyday. In the next few chapters we are going to look at some very practical ways that you can do this with your kids.

2. *Jesus believed in His disciples' spiritual potential:* Jesus made a habit of letting His disciples know that He believed in

them. He modeled this belief over and over again. His decision to leave the mission in their hands after His death was the greatest example of this. In the same way, you are going to need to understand the Holy Spirit-filled potential of your children. Not only do you need to grasp this, but you also need to let them know that you do. Let them know that they matter in the Kingdom.

3. *Jesus called His disciples into the deep water:* Jesus was not satisfied with shallow-water faith. At every appropriate opportunity, and always within the guidance of the Holy Spirit, Jesus called His disciples into a deeper level of spirituality. Jesus, time and time again, let His disciples experience true life in God. Initially, He was always by their side, but little by little He began to give them the keys to the old spiritual Buick. It was only in this way that they came to truly know the faith for themselves. Your kids need the same parenting from you.

Getting There

Take an honest look at your goals for your child. Have you been satisfied with raising a good kid?

Have you prayed to God about His vision for your child's future? Or have you asked Him to bless the one you have predetermined? This week spend some time asking God to show you things about your child that you don't already know. Ask Him how you might lead your kids in the way of His intention. Psalm 139 is a great searching psalm. Pray over this psalm with your child in mind, and then wait for God to speak to you in silence, writing down anything you hear in the journal you created.

In the journal you started for the previous chapter, begin to make notes of what God makes you aware of in regard to your children. What do their names mean? Are you beginning to see the formation of spiritual gifts? What are they?

Spend time with your children, dreaming up a service-oriented project of your own. Try a one-time event. You don't have to commit for life. Just be faithful and go where God leads. Trust in God's ability to change your children's hearts no matter what their ages.

Finally, slow down! Extremes are easy. Whenever I read a book that calls me to a different way, I want to start right away. I want to get radical. If you are a person like that, I challenge you to slow down and let these ideas settle in the depths of your soul for a week or two. God does not need another spiritual New Year's Resolution. Pray to God to confirm this teaching. Remember that the Word of God tells you to test everything (see 1 Thess. 5:21).

Notes

1. Willi Unsoeld (October 5, 1926–March 4, 1979) was an American mountaineer who, along with Tom Hornbein, were members of the first American expedition to summit Mount Everest on May 22, 1963.
2. "San Gorgonio Mountain," Wikipedia.org, September 2, 2010. http://en.wikipedia.org/wiki/San_Gorgonio_Mountain.
3. "Everest Base Camp," Wikipedia.org, September 10, 2010. http://en.wikipedia.org/wiki/Everest_Base_Camp.
4. Dan Loumena, "Big Bear Lake's Jordan Romero, 13, Becomes Youngest Person to Scale Mount Everest," May 21, 2010. http://latimesblogs.latimes.com/outposts/2010/05/big-bears-jordan-romero-becomes-youngest-person-to-scale-mt-everest.html.
5. For more information, see www.brittmerrick.com and www.biggodbook.com.
6. I have actually found that the majority of believers I meet are somewhat unclear in this area for themselves, let alone their children.
7. The Greek word for "infancy" is *paidion* (*pahee-dee -on*), Strong's #3813, meaning, "a childling (of either sex), i.e. (properly), an infant, or (by extension) a half-grown boy or girl; figuratively, an immature Christian: —(little, young) child, damsel."
8. C. S. Lewis, *Mere Christianity* (San Francisco: HarperSanFrancisco, 2001).

CHAPTER

4

Spiritual Arson

A child is not a vase to be filled but a fire to be lit.
FRANÇOIS RABELAIS

Fire season in California is no joke. Every year from about September through November, we hold our collective breaths and wait for the rains and the end of the Santa Anas—strong, hot winds that blow off the desert, turning any small spark into a firestorm.

When it comes to fighting these fires, the key is "containment." Every report of a fire's status is always tagged with a percentage of containment. Containment under 70 percent is never good news.

Your family's life in Christ is a fire that burns deep in the forest of your souls. The devil's primary aim is to keep this fire contained. When your life in Christ is kept within the confines of spiritual places like church services and quiet times, there is a chance that the fires of your spiritual life are close to containment.

The devil does not care if you go to church and have a thousand quiet times a day as long as your life in Christ never breaks those lines to burn into the other areas of your being.

Scripture says that our God is a consuming fire:

Therefore, since we are receiving a kingdom that cannot be shaken, let us be thankful, and so worship God acceptably with reverence and awe, for our "God is a consuming fire" (Heb. 12:28-29).

God wants His presence and His Spirit to roar through your family's life and ignite the embers lying in the family hearth into a permanently blazing fire. This is what happened to Peter. Before Peter left his nets to follow Jesus into the deep water, you can be sure he had a nice little campfire burning in the rock ring of his soul. After all, he was a good Jewish man. He went to synagogue and attended all the high holy days, but that is pretty much where it ended. That is, until Jesus showed up while Peter was fishing and offered him something more; until Jesus began to stoke the fire within.

Remember, God's fire is fire you *don't* want to contain! One of the ways to check the level of containment of God's fire in your family is to survey the map of your life and see which, if any, areas are on fire. First of all, being on fire does not mean that you are raising the dead every day and seeing tongues of fire over your kids' heads. I think that too many of us judge our spirituality by the radical events or emotions that are sometimes attached to different seasons of our spiritual life. Instead, being on fire means that God is a part of all the different segments of your life. He is not compartmentalized. It means that you are aware of Jesus in these different moments and places that fill your life and are responding to His movements. If you are healing the sick, that is great. If you are keeping your patience when standing in line with a rowdy two-year-old, then awesome. Both are equally important and show that God is burning beyond containment in your life.

Here is a quick containment check: Are you and your kids aware of what God is doing in their school or nursery? Do you have a sense of what God's purpose is in that place and how you can fulfill it? When you drive to your daily errands, is the car often full of chaos or are there moments when it becomes a sanctuary? I'm not saying that you need to re-create Westminster Abby, but I would assert that being in the car with your kids is one of the primary environments of your life. If you rarely display the marks of the risen Christ there, you are missing out on a very spiritually fertile ground.

Here's another check: How much of your conversation during any given day is about God? Do stories of God's grace and mercy weave in and out of your conversations? If someone were to overhear your conversations for a day, would they know that you are a son or daughter of the living God?

What about this: Do your children know how to hear from God? Do they sometimes pause to let you know they are hearing an invitation from God into deeper waters? Do they know the Word of God? Do they pray when you are not looking or without your requesting it? Are they concerned for the poor?

All the things I have just mentioned are marks of the Christian life, of a Christian home. If these things are not a regular part of your family life, don't be alarmed; they were not familiar to the early disciples at first, and the disciples ended up changing the world! The question we need to answer as we move forward is, how do we help our family's spiritual fire break the lines of containment?

The only way to do this is to become a spiritual arsonist. Just as Samson set the tails of foxes on fire and released them into the dry grain (see Judg. 15:4), you are going to learn to invite God into the fuel of your life. One thing you can be sure of is that fire will always devour any fuel it is given.

Where Do We Go from Here?

Whenever our family goes on a road trip, our kids pester us to know where we are going and how long it will be until we get there. These are fair questions. Let me rephrase that—these are fair questions when they aren't asked 324 times in a two-hour time span! This would be a good time to answer those questions for you. This book began with the metaphor of life as a journey and that navigating the road of parenting is not for the faint of heart. So, before we go any further on our little metaphorical road trip together, I want to give you a sense of where we have been and where we are going.

The first leg of the journey was about being parents who are committed to seeing life change in our children through what I term gas-pedal parenting. This is simply allowing our children to learn about the fullness of faith through experience; letting them get behind the wheel of their spiritual lives and not parent them in a spirit of fear.

Next, we focused on an important travel condition: the need to get our understanding of a child's spiritual ability in line with Scripture. The point is that if you don't believe in your children's ability and calling from the Lord, they are more likely to not discover it until after they leave home, having never been discipled. The possible outcome with this is that you might be raising only good, moralistic kids instead of kids who have an authentic relationship with Jesus.

In the last thousand words or so, I have written about letting the spiritual fire of God consume the entirety of your life. As we move forward on this journey, I will do my best to give you practical tools to set your family's lives alight.

As we drive forward, let's keep the truths of Luke 5 visible in our rearview mirror. What we see is how Jesus met the disciples where they were and aligned their daily life with the Word of God; how He taught them to really fish; and how He invited them into deeper waters. Let's keep those principles in mind for our children as we continue to gain understanding of how to navigate life as Christian parents.

Understanding—the Key to Change

I have found that when I get just a few tips on spiritual living, they only last a few weeks until the passion fades or I find the next new book. Understanding has always made the difference for me. The books that change me to the core are the ones that change the way I see God and the world. Once my understanding is changed, God's fire singes me forever.

This is why I believe that understanding is the key to living deeply in Christ. When we look at Scriptures we see that there are three ways we know God with our minds. They are wisdom, knowledge and understanding. Wisdom knows what to do. Knowledge knows how to do it. Understanding, on the other hand, lets us know why. Of the three ways of knowing, understanding is the crown jewel, as it incorporates both knowledge and wisdom. It has the ability to change knowledge and wisdom into intimacy.

We know also that the Son of God has come and has given us understanding, so that we may know him who is true. And we are in him who is true—even in his Son Jesus Christ. He is the true God and eternal life (1 John 5:20).

My purpose is that they may be encouraged in heart and united in love, so that they may have the full riches of complete understanding, in order that they may know the mystery of God, namely, Christ (Col. 2:2).

Think about it this way: Jesus died on the cross and you need to ask Him into your heart to be saved. That is wisdom. It is what to do. You move to knowledge by doing something about it—by asking Christ to be the Lord of your life. But it is in grasping the fact of what Christ gave up and how much He loves you that takes you to understanding. All three are important, but living in understanding is what brings me to my knees.

As you continue to read this book, I pray that you do so with a spiritual eye on understanding. What I am *not* offering is a book of parenting tips. Sure, I have some parenting pointers to share, but it is my prayer that you and your kids might have your minds transformed! Once you gain understanding, any pointers and tips for living are easy and will flow naturally.

Key Understandings

Here are some of the key phrases you will find along the way in the rest of this book. I hope they will act as rest stops for you on those long journeys—places you can stop and stretch your spiritual legs while taking in the grandeur of knowing God together as a family.

Key Phrases in the Rearview Mirror

Gas-pedal parents: A gas-pedal parent understands that fullness of faith is found through experience. A gas-pedal parent believes that letting children get behind the wheel of their spiritual life creates children who know God, as opposed to knowing about Him.

Gas-pedal parents also understand that parenting with fear as a foundation is in direct conflict with the Scriptures. God gives us warnings to help us know Him more deeply, not so that we will live in fear.

Deep-water kids: Desiring to raise deep-water kids shows an understanding that children are called to live a faith that matters. In Christ they have been called to bring the kingdom of God to earth. They have the capacity to do amazing things if their parents learn to foster that aptitude and attitude.

Non-compartmentalized spirituality (spiritual arson): Embracing spiritual arson shows an understanding that God desires to set the "all" of your life ablaze. It is a desire to let God break the confines of the usual spiritual places.

Key Phrases on the Road Ahead

Oral tradition (conversation): This represents an understanding that words are one of the primary discipleship tools you have. This is especially true for prayer. Before the written Word of God and iPhone apps existed, the story of God was passed down through the spoken word. A primary way this was done was within the family unit (see Deut. 6). What you speak about is a large part of who you are.

Awareness and recognition: This is the understanding that God is in every moment. It is a wider understanding of what God is saying in the world and how your family fits in. Believers who hear from God are believers who are aware. They are believers who use their spiritual eyes rather than worldly ones to see God in the extravagant as well as the mundane.

Invitation: When we hear from God, it always comes with an invitation. And every time we hear from God, we are at a junction of faith. This is about teaching your kids how to walk in the Spirit.

Key Phrases for Family "Car" Talk

"Prayer is always the answer." (This shows your children a reliance on prayer before action.)

"They can't dig if I'm always holding the shovel" or "Here, you dig." (This is about letting your kids get their spiritual hands dirty.)

"Was the Bible alive for me (us) today?"

"Is the love of Jesus supreme in this decision?" (Using God's Word and 1 Corinthians 13 as a guide for decision making.)

Getting There

In the journal you have created, make a list of the places in your life where God is red-hot. Maybe this is bedtime prayer. Perhaps it is in your Saturday morning Bible reading and pancake time. This is anywhere that you and your children regularly experience God in your lives.

Next, write down the places in your life where you don't think about God much. Maybe it's at the store or at your child's sports practice. Identify ways to bring God into those times. Here are some ideas:

- *Have a verse for the day.* Bring up that verse whenever something in your day reminds you of it. If you commit to this, God will bring these thoughts to you. That's a guarantee.

- *Bring thankfulness into your conversations.* When you are shopping, let your kids know how thankful you are for being able to go to a store and get food. Thanksgiving is a great way to teach your kids to bring God into all of life.

- *Turn your car into a sanctuary.* Get age-appropriate music (for your kids) that honors God, and play it. We let our kids have control of what we listen to in the car 80 percent of the time. This is under the condition that what you listen to is life- and faith-building.

- *Leave 20 minutes early to an appointment with your kids.* Stop at the park, get out and read a Bible story. Talk about it over a chocolate bar and then head to the appointment. Do this regularly. Bible reading times are not only for church and morning quiet times!

Seeing Him:

Finding Jesus in the Everywhere of Your Family's Life

How Jesus and I Changed My Sister's Life
by Lily Stadtmiller

I am going to tell you how my two-year-old sister came to love Jesus. One night, I was telling my sister about how Jesus died on the cross and how to accept Him. I prayed with her, and she did accept Jesus. Now she prays every night.

CHAPTER 5

While They Were Fishing

We worry about what a child will become tomorrow,
yet we forget that he is someone today.
STACIA TAUSCHER[1]

In January 2007, a man walked into the Washington, DC, metro station during rush hour. In his hand was a violin case. He set the case on the ground, pulled out the instrument and began to play.

One by one, passengers who were caught up in a busy rush hour passed by. After three minutes, a middle-aged man stopped for just a few seconds before hurrying on. A minute later the man with the violin received his first dollar tip. This went on for a half hour or more. It is estimated that in that span of time more than 1,000 people passed the musician as he played.

Not long before he finished, a woman who was passing by noticed something unique and stopped. For 10 minutes she sat mesmerized, barely moving, swept away by what she was seeing and hearing. She stood in the middle of the busiest part of the station, unaffected as hundreds of people were forced to walk around her as she listened. Spurred on by her interest, a few more passengers began to stop and stare.

After finishing the last of six selections of Bach, the man finally lowered his instrument. All those who had been listening continued on their way. That is, all except the woman, who looked at the man and said, "I saw you last night at the Library of Congress. It was fantastic."

The man playing that morning in the Washington, DC, metro was none other than Joshua Bell. Bell is one of the most accomplished violinists in the world and debuted as a soloist when he was only 14 years old with the Philadelphia orchestra. The violin he played that morning was a 300-year-old Stradivarius violin named the Gibson ex-Huberman and was crafted in 1713, during what is known as Antonio Stradivari's "Golden Era." Bell purchased the instrument for a little less than $4 million.

In the 45 minutes Bell played that day, he collected $32.17 from 27 different people. This was a paltry sum for a man who commands more than a thousand dollars per minute to play.[2]

On the day this event took place, there was a question being asked: Would those who passed by recognize beauty when it was not packaged as such? Would anyone see genius in the mundane? Would anyone stop to take in one of the greatest musicians of our age when everything around him or her was pushing that person to move on?

This story represents what is happening around us spiritually every day. God is constantly at work and at play in the subway station of our life, but we often find ourselves in the role of the rush-hour passengers focusing on a destination and missing the journey.

The woman in the story above was able to recognize Joshua Bell because she had experienced his music the night before. At some time in her life, someone had turned her on to his music. Maybe she had gotten his music for Christmas or happened to see a PBS advertisement squeezed between Arthur and Rick Steves. Whatever happened, it eventually led her to see him perform in person. After that experience, she was easily able to recognize him when everyone else passed him by.

Part of discipling your kids to live deep-water lives is equipping them with the ability to recognize God when they see Him.

Peter and the Dirty Nets

Peter recognized something special happening that day by the Sea of Galilee while he was cleaning his fishing nets. After a night of fruitless fishing, tired and preoccupied, Peter still was able to recognize God on the shore of his life.

Granted, Jesus did get into Peter's boat, but Peter did not have to respond to the call of the Master. He could have thought, *Who is this crazy man getting into my boat?* He could have shrugged it off as a coincidence, continued to clean his nets and asked Jesus to come back later. Instead, Peter knew something was up. Maybe he was expectant. Maybe he was tired of cleaning nets and had been asking God to reveal Himself. Maybe he was looking for the coming Messiah. We will never know the answers to some of those questions, but what we do know is that by the end of that afternoon, Peter's life was changed. He met God along the water's edge, while cleaning nets.

Cleaning Your Nets

Your life is full of nets that need to be cleaned. Driving to school, eating lunch, going to work and keeping on top of your kids' homework are all part of net cleaning. Valuing each of these as a possible life-changing moment allows for the possibility of the fire in your soul to break from its spiritual containment. This capacity to recognize God in the normal ebb and flow of everyday life is what separates families and children who know about God from those who actually know God.

This capacity to recognize God in the normal ebb and flow of everyday life is what separates families and children who know about God from those who actually know God.

The Tragedy of Humankind

Throughout the Bible, we see people who knew about God but did not recognize Him when He stood among them. This is the greatest tragedy of humankind. When God humbled Himself to stand in their midst, even the priests, scribes and teachers of the law knew Him not.

But I tell you, Elijah has already come, *and they did not recognize him,* but have done to him everything they wished. In the same way the Son of Man is going to suffer at their hands (Matt. 17:12, emphasis added).

He was in the world, and though the world was made through him, *the world did not recognize him* (John 1:10, emphasis added).

But when they saw him walking on the lake, *they thought he was a ghost* (Mark 6:49, emphasis added).

So then, how do you shepherd your children to a place where they know God when they see Him? Why not start with John the Baptist?

You, John the Baptist, and Your Kids

John the Baptist was known for a lot of things. Sure he was an eccentric, a man who had a strange fashion sense and a diet that consisted of grasshoppers and honey. Put those elements of John's life out of your mind for a moment. What I want to focus on is his primary purpose in life, and how it relates to yours as a parent.

John the Baptist's purpose was to prepare the way for the coming of the Lord. He did this by letting anyone who would listen know that the kingdom of God was much nearer than they thought. In a way, he was a tour guide that pointed out the signs of Christ's coming. More importantly, he signaled that Christ was near.

The next day John saw Jesus coming toward him and said, "Look, the Lamb of God, who takes away the sin of the world!" (John 1:29).

When he saw Jesus passing by, he said, "Look, the Lamb of God!" (John 1:36).

In these Scriptures, John recognized Jesus and then spoke of His presence, character and nature. Now put yourself in the story. You are John the Baptist and your kids are your followers. Your divine purpose as a parent is to point to Jesus wherever and whenever you recognize Him and His work in the world.

Over and over again, day after day, as you point to the Savior in your midst and speak to His character and nature, your children will begin to recognize Him for themselves. Then one day they will leave to follow Him on their own. This is exactly what happened with Simon Peter's brother Andrew who was one of the two disciples in the following story.

> When he [John the Baptist] saw Jesus passing by, he said, "Look, the Lamb of God!" When the two disciples heard him say this, they followed Jesus. Turning around, Jesus saw them following and asked, "What do you want?" They said, "Rabbi" (which means Teacher), "where are you staying?" (John 1:36-38).

In this example, you can see the model to emulate as discipler of your children. John's disciples left his ministry and teaching to follow Jesus. There was no break in the action; no wandering years before they got their act together. Rather, there was a smooth transition to a life that was committed to following Christ. No one needed to point to the Christ any longer. They knew who He was when they saw Him. Like the lady in the subway, they had seen and experienced Him before.

A Sunday/Wednesday Jesus

There are a host of reasons why many children don't make this type of transition to a life in Christ that is their own, but I have found that not being able to see or experience God in the day-to-day details of life is one of the biggest.

To be sure, this is not the only reason. The spiritual life cannot be summed up in one tidy "key to success." Let's face it, life is difficult, and the waters of spirituality in a fallen world are tumultuous. Even God's Word assures us that the road to the Kingdom is incredibly narrow and full of tribulations.

> But small is the gate and narrow the road that leads to life, and only a few find it (Matt. 7:14).

> Then they [Paul and Barnabas] returned to Lystra, Iconium and Antioch, strengthening the disciples and encouraging them to remain true to the faith. "We must go through many hardships to enter the kingdom of God," they said (Acts 14:22).

A primary reason for children leaving the faith is that they have not learned to experience Jesus in everyday life. Rather, they have been taught to look for Him in the obvious and within the confines of spiritual events and spiritual places. No one has pointed to Jesus in the normalcy of life. They have never seen Jesus in the subway.

King David and the Dancing Man

Not long ago there was a local mobile phone dealer who was trying to raise a little more awareness of their services. To do so, they placed one of those 30-foot blow-up dancing men on the street corner. You know the kind I mean, they look like giant stick figures but have the moves of Michael Jackson.

Passing that street corner for the next three weeks became an event for us. Not only would I get mesmerized by the pop-and-lock capabilities of this master of the dance floor, but my kids would go crazy with chants of "Dancing man, dancing man," sending the car occupants into a frenzy.

One afternoon, as we approached the intersection of the Dancing Man, hoping that the green light would turn red, I had a thought. It concerned David in 2 Samuel 6:14, dancing before the Ark of the Covenant, giving his everything in worship to God.

When we pulled to a stop, I looked at my girls in the mirror and said, "You know, ladies, there was a dancing man in the Bible who could dance better than this guy, and he even danced in his underwear." To be correct, it was a linen ephod, but either way, it still made his wife, Michal, the daughter of Saul, rebuke him for his indecency.

Now, you can imagine that at this point, I had their attention. As we passed by dancing man, I began to tell them about this hero of God's story, a man who loved God so much that he cared not what anyone thought, even if it seemed undignified in the eyes of all who watched.

From then on, dancing man became a greater part of our story. The Word of God had taken something from our lives, as random as a blown-up dancing man, and met us with a spiritual truth while we were cleaning our nets.

Making an Impression

Perhaps Peter was able to recognize God in the mundane because, as a Hebrew, he had been taught to do so since he was a child. It was part of normal Jewish thought and understanding. Still, it might not be part of yours. Let's take a quick look at Old Testament parenting to see if we can gain some clues.

You are most likely familiar with the Shema even if you don't know it by name. The Shema is a grouping of Scriptures in the Old Testament that were so central to Jewish thought and spiritual life that they were repeated twice every day in Jewish prayer services. These verses were so crucial to Hebrew theology and life that Jesus, when asked what it took to inherit eternal life, pointed to the Shema, quoting Deuteronomy 6:5: "Love the LORD your God with all of your heart and with all of your soul and with all of your strength."

Now at this point, you might be asking yourself, *What does that have to do with net cleaning?* To answer that, we need to read a little further to find the way in which the hearers of this command were encouraged to communicate its truth. It continues:

These commandments that I give you today are to be upon
your hearts. Impress them on your children. Talk about them
when you sit at home and when you walk along the road,
when you lie down and when you get up (Deut. 6:6-7).

The "how to" of this passage lies in the words "impress" and
"talk." The hearers of the Shema are told to create an impression on
their children, to leave a mark. It was a mark that was to be left
through what they talked about as they experienced life together . . .
for example, while they were cleaning fishing nets.

For Moses, the writer of the Shema, it was all about storytelling
in the net-washing moments of life. In essence, Moses was prompting his readers to blend the story we find in God's Word with the
story God is writing in our personal lives. The Shema challenges us
to speak about God, His Word and His actions—when we are at
home, at the dinner table, walking to the park, getting ready for bed
and waking up in the morning . . . all the time. The Shema is to the
Old Testament what "praying without ceasing" (see 1 Thess. 5:17) is
to the New Testament. In these Scriptures we see a challenge to
blend the kingdom of God and His Word into the very fabric of life.

This is really what Christianity and raising Christian children is
all about—recognizing and knowing God and the truth of His Word
in the framework of our everyday life. Our spiritual life is not to be
compartmentalized to the Sabbath and to high holy days. The abun-
dant life in God is to be a part of everything we do.

Believing children who are given the ability to recognize and apply their faith to all situations at anytime are those whose faith runs
deep. It is a deep-water faith, and deep-water faith is daily faith, not
just faith expressed on Sunday mornings and Wednesday nights. It is
the kind of faith that is available to our children when God seems extravagant in His manifest presence and when it feels like He is absent.

Compartmentalizing Jesus

The tendency to compartmentalize your relationship with Jesus is
far more hazardous to the spiritual life of your children than many

of the habits you might consider taboo. Turning on your spiritual senses only when you are in spiritual places or in spiritual need is not the fullness of life the Bible speaks of. I would argue that if this is your habit, you will also find it difficult to find God when you feel you need Him.

Your children acquire the habit of either compartmentalizing their faith or finding it all around them from watching and listening to you. Have you made it a habit to let your life be a place where the kingdom of God and earth meet?

When Life Happens, God Is There

One of the most common challenges I hear when counseling people is that they don't feel as if they ever experience God unless it's in a big "God moment" every so often. The logic for parents then is that if God never speaks to them, how can they point Him out to their children?

Whenever anyone mentions this to me, I respond by asking, "Are you spending time in God's Word and in prayer?" Almost every time, the answer is a resounding no. (We will look at practical and easy ways to change that in the coming chapters.) The next question I ask is, "Are you looking for Him?" The answer I usually hear is that they don't know where to start.

If you think about it, most of us are pretty good at finding the things we desire. When was the last time you had your eye on a new car? Isn't it odd that all of a sudden you see that car everywhere on the road? It feels like there is a secret plot by the auto industry to trail you at all times. Why is this? You know as well as I that it's because you are looking for it. It is what you really want! Desire raises the senses. What you desire, you are aware of. You have set the thing you desire before you. Whatever you desire, you will find. The question is, "What do you desire?" I'm not aware of what the answer is for you in particular, but you can be sure that your children are. They are very aware of what is preeminent in your thinking. If your highest desire is pleasure or wealth, they will pick up on it. If your highest desire is to know God, it will also be evident. The one thing I can guarantee is that you will find what you desire.

> Whom have I in heaven but you? And earth has nothing I desire besides you (Ps. 73:25).

Unless you take a spiritual inventory of your heart and determine that a deeply intimate relationship with Jesus is what you desire most, I suggest that it will be impossible for you to live the life I'm writing about, to become the parent I believe the Bible calls you to be. If you don't desire Jesus supremely, then you will have a very difficult time seeing Him when you are cleaning your nets. You will have an even more difficult time convincing the little disciples who were born to you that the God you talk about is real.

God Communicates to His Children

Let me assure you that God is regularly speaking to you and your kids. Jesus died on the cross so that He might not only save your soul but also open the lines of communication with you. If you make Him first in your family and seek Him, He will be found (see Matt. 7:7). You can take that to the bank!

> But the Counselor, the Holy Spirit, whom the Father will send in my name, will teach you all things and will remind you of everything I have said to you (John 14:26).

> When the Counselor comes, whom I will send to you from the Father, the Spirit of truth who goes out from the Father, he will testify about me (John 15:26).

God is communicating with you in an infinite number of ways. He is communicating in the people you meet, on the roads you drive, during your son's school play and the afternoon practice as you coach your daughter's soccer team. God, through the Holy Spirit, is whispering to you deep in your spirit. He is shouting to you in the sun that just set and in the Bible sitting on your nightstand.

Our good friends the Allens say it this way: "The point is that life happens and God is there."

Train a child in the way he should go, and when he is old he will not turn from it (Prov. 22:6).

If you, as a parent, develop the ability to look for God in every experience, talk about Him, pray through and seek God's Word as a family as life happens, then the Word of God promises that your children will learn how do the same when life happens to them.

Jesus, the Shema and Your Kids

Like Peter, Jesus was a product of Jewish culture and spirituality. He saw God in every moment and made His understanding palatable to His disciples. Over and over again, in the form of conversation, recorded for us to read in the four Gospels, Jesus would point to what surrounded Him and create links from the nature of God to the lives of His followers.

In Mark 4, we see Jesus referencing everything from farmers sowing crops to mustard seeds and even lamps set under bowls. Mark shows us that much of what the disciples learned from Jesus came from His ability to relate the kingdom of God to everyday life in the form of story.

He taught them many things by parables (Mark 4:2).

Crucial to this style of teaching His disciples was Christ's determination to draw away from the crowds afterward and explain to His disciples the parallels to God's kingdom. He drew conclusions and asked questions, hoping to prompt His disciples to develop a faith that was their own. He wanted them to have a faith they would live out when He was no longer with them.

The Jesus Approach

Jesus was consistent in teaching His disciples as much as they could understand.

> With many similar parables Jesus spoke the word to them, as much as they could understand. He did not say anything to them without using a parable. But when he was alone with his own disciples, he explained everything (Mark 4:33-34).

In this Scripture you see four things that Jesus did in regard to using story to train and raise up His disciples:

1. Jesus used stories (parables) based on His awareness of the life that surrounded them.
2. Jesus drew a conclusion to each of His stories by relating them to the truth of God's Word.
3. Jesus taught His disciples up to the point of their understanding.
4. Jesus spent time alone with the disciples, instructing them and explaining the deeper truths of God in a way they could understand.

Incorporating Jesus' Style into Your Parenting Style

Ask God to make you aware of a story, event or happening from your daily life or from the lives of your children that you can use to share something about Him or His kingdom.

Ask the Holy Spirit to counsel you in regard to how Scripture relates to that insight.

> But the Counselor, the Holy Spirit, whom the Father will send in my name, will teach you all things and will remind you of everything I have said to you (John 14:26).

As you find your children's capacity to understand and grasp these spiritual truths, be careful not to teach them beyond their understanding or ability to receive. Meet them at that level. (More on this in later chapters.)

Like Jesus with His disciples, draw away with them from the hubbub of other activities and take the time, individually or as a group, to bring the topic up again later for the purpose of going a little deeper. You don't have to go to a mountaintop to do this. A quiet moment is all you need. Be especially aware of timing. Jesus was always aware of God's timing. Remember, Jesus did not force-feed God's teaching to His disciples.

Getting There

In Psalm 16, David wrote that he had set the Lord before him. For David, God was not found only on the days he went to the temple. Rather, David was a man who made God primary. I guess you could say that David found God in the metro every day. Now it's your turn.

> I have set the LORD always before me. Because he is at my right hand, I will not be shaken (Ps. 16:8).

Here are some ways to expand your faith, and your children's faith, every day:

1. **Take it to the streets**. Start the habit in your car. For the next seven days look for God while you drive. Be especially aware of last Sunday's sermon or your morning devotional readings. God will often weave these into your daily life.

2. **Be a John the Baptist**. When you find a correlation between life and God's Word, bring it to the attention of your kids. It works like this: "Hey, kids, do you see that homeless man over there? Last Sunday, Pastor Mark

spoke about how Jesus was a homeless man. Can you believe that? Why do you think that was?"

3. **Keep track**. Take your journal wherever you go this week. Write down whenever you sense God is in your midst. Sometimes it will be a prompting to help someone pick up dropped groceries. Another time it might be to pray for a person you see on the street, and so on.

4. **You don't have to be right**. Ask the kids what they think God is saying. Write it down in front of them, so they know that you value what they are hearing from God. Affirm them in their hearing.

When you think you hear from God, don't be intimidated that you might not be right. There is no sin in thinking something might be God. I often tell my children, "Hey, I think God is saying this to me. I'm not sure, but here is what I think I heard. What do you guys think?" The point is, when you do this, God has been set before them. He is in the conversation. He is in the story, and you are not even in church. Go figure.

Notes

1. Stacia Tauscher, the attributed author of this quote, is a bit of an anomaly. Many websites list her as a writer, but no one has ever located a title of any book she wrote. There is a possibility that she was an author is the late 1600s, based on another quote attributed to her that incorporates pre-nineteenth century grammar: "A child is a beam of sunlight from the Infinite and Eternal, with possibilities of virtue and vice—but as yet unstained."

2. You can view this event on YouTube by searching for "Josh Bell Subway."

The Heavens Declare His Glory

By reading the Scriptures I am so renewed that all nature seems renewed around me and with me. The sky seems to be a pure, a cooler blue, the trees a deeper green. The whole world is charged with the glory of God and I feel fire and music under my feet.

THOMAS MERTON

It can be argued that no artist has ever left a deeper impression of his personal self through the expression of the self-portrait than Rembrandt. From the outset of his career in the 1620s, to the year of his death in 1669, Rembrandt produced more than 90 self-portraits.

Each of these paintings tell a story and chronicle Rembrandt's life from that of a young, brash and jovial artist, to a more sullen, reflective man whose dark, foreboding color palette almost eclipses his features in his later pieces. Some art scholars even argue that the best way for us to know Rembrandt is through a study of his self-portraits.

The Bible tells us that God is fascinated with the self-portrait. Since the beginning of creation He has been rendering work after work so that His people and this world might not only see Him but come to know Him in a personal way.

God is speaking loudly about Himself and His divine nature through His self-portraits. The key to appreciating them is knowing where to look. Once you know where to look, you and your children can begin to study each of these so that you might know Him in a deeper way. This is an important early step in teaching kids to own their faith.

There are many self-portraits the Father has crafted that help us know Him more. For the purpose of this book, I am going to focus on three of these. They are God in creation; the person of Jesus Christ; and the church, or people, of God.

Each of these act as a megaphone of God's presence among us and are easy to access as parents look for ways to bring an awareness of God into the normalcy of everyday family life. Again, think of yourself in the role of a John the Baptist, using every opportunity to make God known to your kids.

Seeing God in Creation

"For since the creation of the world God's invisible qualities—his eternal power and divine nature—have been clearly seen, being understood from what has been made, so that men are without excuse" (Rom. 1:20).

This verse is one of my favorites in the Bible. It espouses a radical truth. Paul is saying that by looking at creation alone, we have enough evidence of a Creator-God to understand His story of redemption. Paul says that even if God never revealed Himself to the Patriarchs, as recorded in the Old Testament, or gave us the Scripture, or sent Jesus into the world, there would still be enough evidence to convict all of mankind in regard to sin. Creation alone tells of God's redemptive place in the world.

I love this verse because it reveals the power of God. Only God can paint a picture that has the power to reveal His divine nature. As a parent, this verse not only inspires me, but it also encourages me to find God in creation and share what I see with Lily and Lucy. My hope, then, is that they will become women of God who see beyond the creation to the Creator, ever mindful of Him by virtue of what is before their eyes every day.

This verse refers to what is known in theological studies as natural revelation. There are two types of revelation God uses in making Himself known to us: *special revelation* and *natural revelation*. Natural revelation is what God shows us about Himself through the created order. Special revelation is knowledge of God and of spiritual matters that can be discovered through supernatural means, such as miracles and the Scriptures. The earthly life of Jesus and the witness of other believers also fall into this category.[1]

The natural revelation of creation can often be a challenge for many believing parents. Many of us have been taught to appreciate God's creation, but not to dig deeper to find meaning for our lives from it. I would say that it has even gone as far as people denying what they see God clearly saying to them in the world around them for fear of stepping out of bounds theologically. Because of this, many have thrown out the baby with the bath water.

Using creation as a pointer to expose the works of God in the world is not only incredibly useful, but also theologically accurate. Jesus often told His disciples to look at what creation was saying in order to see the Father and His work in history. Here is just one example of Christ's use of creation to disciple His future apostles:

> Now learn this lesson from the fig tree: As soon as its twigs get tender and its leaves come out, you know that summer is near. Even so, when you see these things happening, you know that it is near, right at the door. I tell you the truth, this generation will certainly not pass away until all these things have happened. Heaven and earth will pass away, but my words will never pass away (Mark 13:28-31).

Jesus told His disciples to pay close attention to creation, for in it is many insights to how we remain in Christ. My only word of caution is that when you experience insight or direction from God in the world around you, make sure to check what you have discovered against the truth of God's Word. Finding God in nature begins with one foot on the trail and one hand on the Bible. With that said, let's look at some ways we can bring God to the doorstep of our children's daily life.

The Snows of Redemption

Not long ago, Karie and I were channel surfing and came across one of the countless reality shows that are now a staple of the American TV diet.

This show was about dating couples and their hope to find true love. In the course of the show, the couple ended up on a snow-filled mountain somewhere in Canada. As the couple was sitting in the snow-capped mountains, the woman made a fascinating comment that reflected Romans 1:20. She said, "I love the snow. It is so beautiful. It reminds me of forgiveness."

She might not have realized it, but God had spoken to her through natural revelation. He had shown that what had died in the fall, because of the cold, had now been covered up with a blanket of forgiveness, a fresh start. If she were to have stuck around another few months, she would have seen another characteristic of God. It is called spring, and represents new life.

While my girls were not watching this show with us, it would have been a great opportunity for me to pause the DVR and take a moment to discuss the truth that was just presented unknowingly by the woman on the mountain.

This is what I mean by using creation as a tool for creating an awareness of God in every moment. Even though we were in our home that night, watching TV, God was able to use His creation to awaken my spirit to truth. All of a sudden, God was part of Karie's and my down time.

The more you pursue creating an awareness of God through a study of His creation, and you share it with your children, the more He will fill places in your life where and when you least expect it. This will also begin to create a habit in your children of becoming kids who see God when you are not looking.

The Commander and Henry Mancini

One of the many gifts I thank my parents for was their commitment to getting my brother, Albie, and me out into nature. We had a classic 1974 Commander motor home. It was epic. It came complete with a map of the US on the table in the dining area, captain's chairs with a full 180-degree swivel, a loft bed, a ladder on the back so we could go on the roof at night and, of course, my dad's eight-track assortment of Henry Mancini and Frank Sinatra. Okay, we were not tent campers, but it still counts.

Before the age of 10, I stood at the base of giant sequoias, climbed the ladders of Mesa Verde in southwestern Colorado, saw herds of Elk in Wyoming, gazed at the Tetons and watched Old Faithful erupt. The interesting thing is that I don't have lots of memories of my childhood that come back strong. Many of the memories I do have are emotionally traumatic, due to my parents' struggle with alcoholism, but I remember each of these experiences in God's creation vividly and fondly. I must have 30 memories that stand like strong towers in my mind. There is something transcendent in nature, something that brought comfort to a messed-up little kid. That thing was the voice of God.

I sometimes wonder how much more I would have heard if my folks knew how to tell me about the God who stands behind the creation that was touching the fabric of my soul, about what each of these things were saying on an even deeper biblical level.

The Psalms View Creation

The writers of the psalms not only understood these parallels, but they also capitalized upon them as a regular tool for getting the message of God across to the hearts of their listeners. They knew that as they spoke, another voice was echoing their message. It was the voice of God transcendent in creation. You see, creation is just a huge physical metaphor. Like all good metaphors, the psalms accurately describe what they are representing in a language the hearers can understand. Just take a look at Psalm 19:

The heavens declare the glory of God; the skies proclaim the work of his hands. Day after day they pour forth speech; night after night they display knowledge. There is no speech or language where their voice is not heard. Their voice goes out into all the earth, their words to the ends of the world. In the heavens he has pitched a tent for the sun, which is like a bridegroom coming forth from his pavilion, like a champion rejoicing to run his course. It rises at one end of the heavens and makes its circuit to the other; nothing is hidden from its heat.

What the psalmist and other writers of the Bible understood was that God's voice through His creation has a unique way of penetrating to the heart of mankind. There are psalms about water, deserts, deer, mountains, oceans, valleys, skies, eagles and even dirt; and in each of these metaphors are deep biblical truths that you can impress upon your children. Here are just a few.

He [the man who meditates on God's Word] is *like a tree* planted by *streams of water, which yields its fruit in season* and *whose leaf does not wither.* Whatever he does prospers (Ps. 1:3, emphasis added).

Who satisfies your desires with good things so that your youth is *renewed like the eagle's* (Ps. 103:5, emphasis added).

But those who hope in the LORD will renew their strength. *They will soar on wings like eagles;* they will run and not grow weary, they will walk and not be faint (Isa. 40:31, emphasis added).

As the deer pants for streams of water, so my soul pants for you, O God (Ps. 42:1, emphasis added).

Your righteousness is *like the mighty mountains,* your justice like the great deep. O LORD, you preserve both man and beast (Ps. 36:6, emphasis added).

Each of these Scriptures points to a truth about God hidden in the living metaphor of creation. It is that simple. This is a parenting tool that is at your fingertips every day.

Abraham's Future in the Stars

Even God, when speaking to Abraham about the future of his descendents, pointed to the stars as a reference to what He was going to accomplish. I find this really interesting, because even though God was speaking directly to Abraham in a theophany, or direct manifestation of Himself, He still used an outside example or metaphor from creation to drive the point home.

I often wonder why God did not just say, "Hey, I'm God, and I'm going to give you more descendents than you can count." He is God, after all. Is not a voice from heaven or a personal visit enough? Why does He have to back up what He is saying to Abraham with a head nod to the picture of creation?

He took him outside and said, "Look up at the heavens and count the *stars*—if indeed you can count them." Then he said to him, "So shall your offspring be" (Gen. 15:5, emphasis added).

I will surely bless you and make your descendants as numerous as the *stars in the sky* and as the sand on the seashore. Your descendants will take possession of the cities of their enemies (Gen. 22:17, emphasis added).

God used creation when He spoke to Abraham because He wanted to give the patriarch a pivot point or daily reminder regarding His promise about Abraham's descendants. Do you think after God spoke this word over him that Abraham ever looked at the stars in the same way? Creation had now become a constant reminder of what God had declared.

If you are not using God's creation as a crook to shepherd your child's spiritual development, I want to encourage you to start now. Not using creation is like going golfing without a putter, or fishing without a hook. *It is one of the most important weapons in your spiritual parenting arsenal.* It is the method by which Jesus taught His disciples over and over again. If you begin to model this approach, you will be giving your children a gift that will implant in them a constant reminder of who God is whenever they come in contact with the created world around them. More importantly, you will be aligning what they are seeing with the Word of God, making it an integrated part of their everyday lives.

Better Gas Mileage

Many believers struggle with creation as a pivot point for finding God's voice and presence to guide them. The reason for this is that they don't want to be associated with New Age thought or philosophy. Because of this, many have abandoned creation as a discipleship lesson, choosing not to use God's spiritual tool of creation when shepherding their children.

I think this pleases the devil. You see, he is a being of extremes. If he cannot get you to worship creation, then he wants to rob it of its gospel power by tempting you to disregard it. In both of these scenarios, the person in question has been led off the path of God's intention.

Let me reassure you that all truth is God's truth. The problem with worshiping creation over the Creator only begins when creation becomes the focus of intent rather than a pivot point to highlight God Himself. Paul talks about this in Romans 1:25:

> They exchanged the truth of God for a lie, and worshiped and served created things rather than the Creator—who is forever praised.

Here Paul is showing the fork in the road that separates truth from lie. The truth is that God uses creation to give us daily reminders as to who He is and how He works in the world. The lie begins when individuals begin to direct their focus back to the creation rather than the Creator. Creation at this point moves from its purpose as a mirror that reflects God to an image to be worshiped. This is the heart of the New Age movement.

With that said, let me encourage you to grasp God in creation today. Slow down, smell the roses and talk with your children about how we are a fragrance to God (see 2 Cor. 2:15). Watch the sunrise and speak of God's new mercies that are fresh every morning (see Lam. 2:22). Instill in your children a love for God and His creation and, in so doing, move them one step closer to being kids who experience and know God when you are not looking.

Getting There

This week, read Genesis 1 and 2 to your kids. If you have really young children, use the kids' picture Bible. Challenge them to find three interesting things in the story and talk about it. You might be surprised at what they find.

Get out into God's creation. This week take your kids somewhere that speaks of God. This can be the park, a botanical garden in the middle of your busy city, the local mountains or even the roof of your home at night. Once you are there, bring God into the conversation. Talk about His glory, how He created the things you see around you. If you have very young children, I still encourage you to do this. God has the ability to touch the soul of a child beyond his or her cognitive ability. A great example of this is found in John the Baptist's leaping in his mother's womb when hearing the news of the coming birth of the Savior (see Luke 1:41-45).

Look up as many Scriptures as you can about creation. (This can easily be done with a good Internet search engine or Bible concordance.) Familiarize yourself not only with the analogy but also with the corresponding truth. If you're with your children when God points these out to you, pass it on. Make sure to focus on the intent behind the metaphor. Remember, creation is an open doorway to hidden spiritual truth.

Note
1. "Special Revelation," Wikipedia.org, July 8, 2010. http://en.wikipedia.org/wiki/Special_revelation.

Jesus and Half Dome

When you stand in Yosemite Valley there is no need for anyone to remind you that there is something in this world bigger than you.
SHELTON JOHNSON[1]

At the center of the state of California is the Yosemite Valley, a national park whose beauty is difficult to match elsewhere within the state and, some would say, the world. It would be easy to imagine that it was Yosemite that majestically called forth the pioneering spirit of expansion to the West. Can you tell I *love* this place?

The central valley at the heart of Yosemite is a natural theme park of sorts. Each towering site is an "E Ticket" attraction. All are breathtaking, from El Capitan, a mighty rock formation, to Bridal Veil Falls, a singular and superlative fan of water cascading from its summit, as its name suggests. This is a place so beautiful and exalting of God's hand in creation that it seems incredibly redundant that a chapel was built on its valley floor.

While all of these sites within Yosemite are magnificent, there is one that stands above the rest. In its shadow the rest are bridesmaids. If you have spent any time taking in the photographic work of Ansel Adams, then you will know I'm speaking of Half Dome.[2]

Any description of this giant granite monolith runs the risk of profaning it. It is that majestic, that splendid and that grand. We took Lily there for the first time when she was four. We did it all on that trip. We sat in the meadows of Tuolumne, ate as deer grazed only feet from us and watched as Yosemite Falls pounded the valley floor with vigor. We were content and having the time of our lives. Then we rounded the corner and saw the sun's red half-light brilliant against the massive flat face of Half Dome. We were frozen with awe and must have looked like the proverbial "deer in the headlights."

Do you know what you do when you see Half Dome for the first time? You stop right there on the trail or pull the car over, and stand gawking. If you have been there, you know what I mean.

When Lily saw Half Dome, it changed her. For more than six months after we got home from our trip, she referenced the rock face every time she saw any rock that resembled it. She even found a palm-size replica at the beach that she still has. Four years later, if you ask her to draw Half Dome, she can do it, even though we have not returned there since she first saw it. It is kind of like what happened when she got her first look at Jesus.

Seeing Jesus

It was the fifth night in a row that our then three-year-old daughter, Lily, had asked us to read her the story of Jesus' death on the cross. From the time she was born, we had been reading to her at bedtime from a children's picture Bible. We had read through the crucifixion story before, but for some reason this time was different.

On the third night, I started to get concerned. Even for a children's Bible, the pictures were pretty realistic. I wondered if the topic of Jesus' crucifixion was too much for this preschooler.

A couple weeks later, we were driving home in our car when the subject of the cross came up again. Near the end of the conversation, we asked Lily if she wanted to ask Jesus to live in her heart and wash it clean. She said, "No, not right now." I was surprised at her answer. I have experienced that most children will do something like this just because their parents have asked them. But always conscious of our desire for our children to have a faith of their own, we left it at that. Let's just say that, like Mary, Karie and I stored and treasured these things up in our hearts (see Luke 2:19).

Two weeks later, on the way home from school, Lily asked us if we wanted to hear a secret. When we said that we did, Lily told us that she had asked Jesus to come into her heart. For two weeks, Lily had been pondering the question of Jesus on her own. In her own timing, and without us there, she made a decision to follow Christ.

What blew us away was that God had done something in Lily's three-year-old heart when we were not looking. Lily, however, had been looking. She was looking at Jesus, in the same way that millions of tourists stare up at Half Dome from Yosemite's valley floor.

This instance was the first of many that showed us that our daughter was developing a personal faith. It was a faith that was being transformed by what she was looking at. While Karie and I had always wanted this for our children, we never set out with a game plan to make it happen. Rather, God, in His faithfulness, created a path. All we did was try to give Lily opportunities to gaze. We have done our best to pull over to the side of any spiritual road we see.

A Glimpse of Jesus

We don't start any family road trip without first knowing where we are going. This principle can be applied to parenting, except that the destination we are heading toward is always Jesus. His glory is the final destination of every decision we make.

While it is true that our children will chart a different faith journey than ours, there is one key element in creating a deep faith in them that is common to all. That essential ingredient is *the power of the gospel of Jesus Christ*. Without a clear knowledge of the gospel and daily engagement with it, there is little hope that you or your children will ever live spiritually potent lives. Your children might never even make it out of the driveway.

I am not ashamed of the gospel, because it is the power of God for the salvation of everyone who believes: first for the Jew, then for the Gentile. For in the gospel a righteousness from God is revealed, a righteousness that is by faith from first to last, just as it is written: "The righteous will live by faith" (Rom. 1:16-17).

For Lily, life change happened when she got a glimpse of Jesus. It caused her to pull over and gaze at His life and redemptive work on the cross. God supernaturally reached beyond Karie's and my ability, and touched our daughter with the story of the ages, and her eyes met His.

I had experienced this transformation at the age of 12. Karie found Jesus as a very young child and has no definitive date as to her conversion. Jesus was just always there. My mother turned to Jesus at the late age of 49, after being set free from 30 years of alcoholism; and for my father, it was on his death bed.

As a matter of fact, every member of my extended family who is walking with God all had an experience with Jesus. Each were given a glimpse of the God-Man who walked among us, and that is what changed their lives. If your children are also to find a faith that lasts, they too will need to meet and fall in love with Jesus. His birth, death and resurrection will need to become part of every day and every mile.

Jesus Is the Final Word!

The book of Hebrews tells us that God has spoken to us in all sorts of ways throughout the ages, but there is one word that brings everything together and is the culmination of His revelation:

In the past God spoke to our forefathers through the prophets at many times and in various ways, but in these last days he has spoken to us by his Son, whom he appointed heir of all things, and through whom he made the universe. The Son is the radiance of God's glory and the exact representation of his being, sustaining all things by his powerful word. After he had provided purification for sins, he sat down at the right hand of the Majesty in heaven (Heb. 1:1-3).

Jesus is God's final word (see John 1:1)! There is nothing more that needs to be said. He is the totality of all wisdom and knowledge (see Col. 2:2-3). Everything we need (and our children need) is wrapped up in the person of Jesus Christ!

While your children may have already been introduced to Jesus, what I want to do in this chapter is help you move your son or daughter from a knowledge of Him to an intimacy and dependence upon Him. You see, for Jesus to stick, He has to become alive to them in a way they can't deny.

Donuts and Adult Bible Study

When I was 12, I ended up at Skyline Wesleyan church in Lemon Grove, California, not far from San Diego. You might have heard of this church; it was where John Maxwell was pastor before he went on to become a well-known author and speaker in the leadership arena.

On the first weekend we were there, I knew that something was weird. They gave away donuts after Sunday School. That was enough for me to want to stay. When I came out of the class that day, I found my mom crying on the front steps of the church. Maxwell, a traveling evangelist at the time, had preached on having a loving Father in God. For a woman with an abusive father, this was a big stretch for my mom, but one that God was able to bridge.

We came back that Sunday night, as eventually became our custom. At some point in the course of the evening, John gave an altar call. My brother, who is four years older, went down front first. I followed out of curiosity. Before I knew it, John was holding my hands and praying with me for salvation. I didn't really feel much at the time but would come to find that it stuck.

The next week, my mother decided to attend a new class starting on Sunday mornings called "The Life of Jesus." Instead of going back to the donut class, I asked my mother if I could come to her class. Why I did this I will never know. Mind you, I was only 12.

The class was on the book of John. If there was a person under 40, I did not see them. Still, the teaching and the study captivated me. Somewhere during the six weeks that we attended the class, Jesus became real to me. I don't know how else to explain it than to say that, like John Wesley, "My heart became strangely warmed."

While I have many times since then sensed Christ's presence, it is this particular experience that stands out. Not only did it plant in me a love for the Word of God, but it also stood like a beacon in times of doubt, always giving me a place of reference to mark when Jesus became real to me.

Getting to the Heart of the Matter

So how do you create a love for Jesus in your children that goes beyond head knowledge? The answer is that you can't. Love for another person is not something that can be given away. Each human being, your kids included, needs to make his or her own choice to love another. What you can do, though, is tell your children of the love that Jesus has for them, making sure that the gospel is lived out in your family life every day.

Scripture is clear that love for Jesus never starts with us. Rather it is Christ who loved us first and our love in return is always a response to His reaching out to us!

> But God demonstrates his own love for us in this: While we were still sinners, Christ died for us (Rom. 5:8).

Knowledge of this fact is the greatest gift you can give your children, and if they are to go on to develop a faith that is their own, it will need to be rooted in a knowledge of Christ's eternal love for them and His work on the cross. This is the gospel. This is what changes lives (see Rom. 1:16). In a sense, you are your children's own personal Billy Graham, and like him, you are going to be relentless in communicating the story of God's love to your kids in a way that is unique to whom God designed them to be.

In the same way that a missionary or church planter needs to understand the culture in which they minister, you are being called to your children's unique mission's field. Your son is different from your daughter and needs to be approached uniquely. If you seek God, He will give you the understanding and perspective on how to do this.

Perhaps for one child, an academic approach to the Scriptures is how that child will personally accept God's truth. For another child, it may be through the time you spend on the trail together in places like Yellowstone and Yosemite. Either way, you are the missionary who is going to introduce each of your children to the love and gospel of Jesus Christ, and God is going to show you how. Have you done this for each of your children, or are you using the same approach no matter how your child is wired? Spiritual parenting like this is like trying to drive from Pittsburgh to San Francisco with only a map of California.

Taught More than Caught

How do kids learn? It goes back to the idea of engagement. For example, how do kids learn to swim? They learn how to swim by being in water. Likewise, if you want to teach your son or daughter to play football, you do so by letting him or her be on the field of play. You don't just buy season tickets—box seats and a rulebook do not create Hall of Fame quarterbacks. If your kids don't get on-the-field experience, it would be ridiculous for you to allow them to take their first snap of the ball in a college game. Yet this is a model I see believing parents repeat over and over when it comes to training their children to live for Christ within the culture—when it comes to instilling a faith within them that is separate from their parents.

One of the many things I give my mother credit for is that when I told her I wanted to go to the adult Sunday School, she said yes. How many parents would have said no, either because they wanted some of their own downtime or failed to believe that a 12-year-old could grasp the Word of God? The answer is: plenty.

In this instance, my mother led me out into the deep water. Like Jesus with Peter, my mother recognized when I was willing to "push the boat a little ways from shore." Mom recognized something that was unique to how God created me and navigated the gospel of Jesus toward it. That is great parenting!

Old School Discipleship

In the last 15 to 20 years, I have noticed a shift in discipleship training in the Western church. There has been a shift of emphasis in regard to the raising up of twenty-first-century disciples. I believe this shift has also affected the way that parents are discipling their children.

I have seen a transition from solid, biblical, hands-on experiential training to a more "caught than taught" model. Discipleship has moved away from a small group of believers experiencing life together with "one hand on the Bible and a foot in the world" to a "let's just hang out and share life together" model.

While community and spending time together are key to spiritual growth, they are not what changes lives to the core. Rather, we are transformed by knowledge of God through His Word. When we implement what we know of Him in His Word (the gospel) into our normal everyday life, He is made real to us.

As we saw a couple chapters ago, this was the pattern of the people of God before Jesus' time. Jewish parents knew that if they were to impress upon their children a personal knowledge of God, it was going to happen because they took personal responsibility to train their children in the law of their great God!

> Only be careful, and watch yourselves closely so that you do not forget the things your eyes have seen or let them slip from your heart as long as you live. *Teach them to your children and to their children after them.* Remember the day you stood before the LORD your God at Horeb, when he said to me, "Assemble the people before me to hear my words so that they may learn to revere me as long as they

live in the land and may teach them to their children" (Deut. 4:9-10, emphasis added).

The Importance of the Four Gospels

Just as Lily learned about Yosemite by going there, the same is true for knowing Jesus. Your kids will know about Jesus and His kingdom because you take them there, experiencing Him through His Word. Once they know His story, they can blend it into theirs. *This is why the four gospels are where you want to start when it comes to introducing your children to Jesus.* They have the power to change your children from the inside out. As you commit to sharing the Gospels with your children, you will be aided by a supernatural "special revelation" that will go deeper than anything you will ever tell them apart from His Word:

> For the word of God is living and active. Sharper than any double-edged sword, it penetrates even to dividing soul and spirit, joints and marrow; it judges the thoughts and attitudes of the heart (Heb. 4:12).

The Gospels are especially relevant to children because they are story, and the language of children is story. In the Gospels, not only do we read about life situations that Jesus faced, but we also find out how He dealt with these situations in action and attitude. In each of these instances there is a lesson wrapped in a story.

With this in mind, you want to rely heavily on these four books when reading the Bible to your kids. I would encourage you to set a goal of reading through the four Gospels once or twice per year. You can do this every night at bedtime or during your family's morning breakfast ritual.

Put Your Kids in the Story

When we read the Word to our kids, we need to make sure that it comes alive for them. While I believe that God's Word will never return void without accomplishing its purpose (see Isa. 55:11), it still needs to be broken down so that it has a better chance of hitting its mark.

Recently, I had the privilege of meeting pastor and author Eugene Petersen and hearing him speak on the topic of the gospel and story. One of his main points was that if he could rearrange seminary curriculum for pastors in training he would make the first year or more devoted to the art of storytelling.

Dr. Peterson spoke about how story and especially movies are the common language of our day. He mentioned how the best movies allow us to enter into the story, to see ourselves as the characters and feel what they feel.

Dr. Petersen drove this point home with a very powerful illustration about his own grandchildren. He mentioned how when his grandchildren were little, he would tuck them in at night with fantastical stories he made up. One night his grandchild looked up and said, "Grandpa, put me in the story, put me in the story." From that point on his grandchildren became central characters in that night's story.

I bring this up because it is exactly what you will want to do when you are reading the Gospels to your children. In essence, you want to put them into the story. Here's how you do it. Let's say you are reading the following passage:

> One day as he was teaching, Pharisees and teachers of the law, who had come from every village of Galilee and from Judea and Jerusalem, were sitting there. And the power of the Lord was present for him to heal the sick. Some men came carrying a paralytic on a mat and tried to take him into the house to lay him before Jesus. When they could not find a way to do this because of the crowd, they went up on the roof and lowered him on his mat through the tiles into the middle of the crowd, right in front of Jesus (Luke 5:17-19).

First, look at the setting. Ask your children to picture the setting in their heads. Ask them what it looks like. Kids have great imaginations; let them paint a picture for you. What was the roof like? What was Jesus wearing? Just as an artist interprets a gospel scene onto a canvas, your kids are going to do the same with words and imagination.

Next, ask them about the characters in the story. What people were there? What were they doing? Were the Pharisees there? What about the men on the roof . . . what were they doing? Do you think Jesus got annoyed that these guys were interrupting His teaching?

Remember, there is not a character in Scripture that is not there for an eternal purpose. All of them tell the story and play a part in what God is communicating in the story as a whole.

You may even want to give your kids the opportunity to see the story from the perspective of the different characters. Sometimes I'll say, "Okay, Lily, you are a Pharisee, what are you thinking right now?" Or, "You're the man being lowered through the roof. Are you afraid that Jesus will get mad at you? What are you thinking, and what did you think after He healed you?"

By doing this kind of thing, you will help make the Scriptures come alive to your kids and allow the Holy Spirit to speak and elaborate upon the Scriptures in the depths of their souls.

Is this not what your favorite Bible teachers do? Think about it. Who are your favorite preachers? I would imagine that each of them has the ability to make you part of the story and, more importantly, help you understand the intentions behind the actions.

The Why Behind the What

Do you know anyone who has been encouraged by the acrostic WWJD? (What Would Jesus Do?) Maybe you have even worn the bracelet. While this Christian cultural icon asks a tremendous question, I think its makers should market another wristband for the accompanying arm that reads WDJDI. It would stand for Why Did Jesus Do It?

Understanding the "why" behind the "what" is the most important element of Scripture. And that is why just reading the Scriptures to your children is not enough. In the end, you want to give them an understanding of the message behind the words. For instance, Jesus died on the cross; but why He died on the cross is what changes lives. Jesus died for us because of His great love for us. Understanding is what gets to the heart of a matter. Understanding is what changes attitudes.

> By wisdom a house is built, and through understanding it is established (Prov. 24:3).

You can build a home with wisdom, but it will last because of understanding.

The "why" is what will lead your children from a knowledge of Jesus' actions to understanding His heart. When we begin to understand the heart of God, following Him and trusting Him with our lives becomes easier to do. It is also what will establish the spiritual home you are trying to build within your kids.

Thus, when you read the Gospels to your children, you will want to pause after each story and ask questions that get to the heart of the story. "Why did Jesus stop alongside the road to help the blind man? Why did Jesus not get mad at the woman who poured out a year's worth of wages when she anointed His feet with perfume?" "Why did Jesus forgive Peter after Peter denied Him three times?"

Bringing It Home in the Everyday

The time you spend reading and understanding the Gospels will become deeply practical when shepherding your children through the joys as well as the difficulties of life. By committing yourself to a knowledge of the heart of Jesus as shown in His Word (especially in the Gospels), you will find a wealth of power, wisdom and understanding to navigate life.

When your child comes home from school after being made fun of, you can reference how not only Jesus was made fun of, but also how He reached out to those who were considered outcasts and has a special love for them. When your child struggles with making a tough decision, you can point to how Jesus called Peter out into the storm to walk on water so that he would one day have the courage to lead an entire Church.

In this way, you will blend the story and heart of Jesus into the daily lives of your children. You make Him knowable. It will be as if you have pulled off the road of life to let your kids get out and stand silent in awe. And they will be changed by what they see.

Calling Others from Their Nets

Not long ago, Lucy walked out of her room in the morning clinging to Blue Bear. (You will learn more about him later.) She was clad in her usual pull-ups, as we can't get her to keep any clothes on. Let's just say that she lives life *al fresco*.

This particular morning she walked out and the first thing that came out of her mouth was, "Jesus in my heart." Karie and I had no idea what she meant. Yes, we know what "Jesus in my heart" means, but we didn't know why she was saying it. Up to this point, we had not formally discussed with her asking Jesus to be Lord of her life. Karie inquired what she was talking about. Just then, Lily walked out of the room they share and said, "Oh yeah, last night we were up talking and I told her all about Jesus, and how He died on the cross for our sins and how she could go to heaven. Then I asked if she wanted to pray with me. I prayed with her, and now she has Jesus in her heart."

Not only was this moment anointed, it was just classic Lily. There she went again, doing spiritual stuff when we weren't looking, having a life in Christ on her own. She took the old spiritual Buick out for a spin and invited her little sister to ride shotgun.

The amazing thing is that Lucy has been a very different toddler since Lily led her to Jesus. Do we believe it was a legitimate conversion? Yes, we do. The reason why is that we have seen Lucy's entire way of living transformed. She is more loving, kind and less selfish. She loves to pray and can't stop talking about Jesus.

Like Peter and the disciples, Lily was able to call others (her sister, Lucy) out into the deeper water. She knew that Jesus was not stuck in only spiritual places. She was able to see God in a moment and respond. The cool thing is that any kid can do this.

Getting There

If you haven't done this already, introduce each of your children to Jesus. Have you thought about each of their unique personalities and used a different road map for each?

Make the story of Jesus' birth, death and resurrection central to your conversations this week. With the help of the Holy Spirit, weave the story into the normalcy of your life.

This week seek to bring the Gospels to life with your kids. Use a Bible that is relevant to their age and put them into the story. Spend time talking about the characters, the settings and, more importantly, the why behind the what!

In your journal, spend a few minutes developing a yearly gospel-reading plan. This can be done on your own or easily found with a quick search of the Internet for something like "one-year gospel-reading plan."

Watch the story of Jesus. You can find a movie or cartoon on the life of Jesus that is appropriate to the age of your children. You might be able to find this on YouTube, Netflix or a DVD at a local Christian bookstore.

Maybe it's time to share your salvation testimony with your kids. This week, tell your kids in a simple and straightforward way why you love Jesus.

Notes

1. Shelton Johnson is a park ranger at Yosemite Valley Park. See his column at www.pbs.org/engage/blog/ask-park-ranger-shelton-johnson.
2. You can find many of Ansel Adams's photos of Yosemite at www.anseladams.com.

Who Are You Camping With?

*Life is partly what we make it, and partly what it is
made by the friends we choose.*
TENNESSEE WILLIAMS

Our lead pastor, Mark Foreman, has a question he asks himself
when hiring a new staff member: "Would I want to go camping
with these people for a week?" It's a great question that can help
you distinguish the people you want to be with the most. We all
know what it's like to be in the car or even on a road trip with someone who makes you a little uncomfortable or even miserable. This
person seems to have a knack for bringing out the worst in you.
You are called to love him or her, but this person tends to make life
more difficult. When thinking through a church staff, the people
you hire create the DNA of who you are as a staff and as a church.

The same is true for your family. *You are becoming like the people you are surrounded by.* Move to a new city or country and it will
not be long until your way of life, speech and accent changes, a little or a lot.

Let's put this into the context of your kids. The people who
surround your son or daughter on a regular basis influence what
they are becoming. Scripture is clear that they are either being
dragged down or raised up by the company they keep.

Do not be misled: "Bad company corrupts good character" (1 Cor. 15:33).

I long to see you so that I may impart to you some spiritual
gift to make you strong—that is, that you and I may be
mutually encouraged by each other's faith (Rom. 1:11-12).

I have found that parents are usually more concerned about
keeping their kids away from "bad apples" than they are about intentionally placing their children around the people and other
children who build and shape good character.

My parents were very intentional in trying to protect me from
bad influences, but there was not much discussion in regard to
guiding me toward positive influences. Don't get me wrong, I am
sure they wanted this to happen, but it was a more caught than
taught model. It's sort of like planning a vacation by thinking of
all the places you don't want to go. It's a bit backwards.

I want to look at this parenting model in light of relationships.
The Word shows us that individual believers are the representation of God on earth. You have an amazing opportunity to increase the speed of your child's spiritual development based on
who you surround them with.

Christ's Representation on Earth

Individual believers are another profound self-portrait of God, a
special revelation of sorts. Christians are, in fact, the representation of the presence of God on earth as He lives within their hearts
and as they are being conformed to His image.

For we are to God the aroma of Christ among those who
are being saved and those who are perishing (2 Cor. 2:15).

For those God foreknew he also predestined to be conformed to the likeness of his Son, that he might be the
firstborn among many brothers (Rom. 8:29).

It's Not What You Know, It's Who You Know

Think about how you came to know Jesus. I imagine that God showed Himself to you through some key people. Perhaps it was a believing grandparent, a coworker or coach. More likely it was a series of people who came in and out of your life at different places and times. Whether you knew it or not, God was weaving His very presence into the fabric of your life.

As I look back upon my life, much of its direction and meaning has been discovered through the community of believers that God surrounded me with.

As a parent, you co-labor with God by bringing the people of God into the lives of your children. *When you do this, you allow your children to actually spend time with Jesus.* If you don't believe me, just ask Paul.

And we, who with unveiled faces all reflect the Lord's glory, are being transformed into his likeness with ever-increasing glory, which comes from the Lord, who is the Spirit (2 Cor. 3:18).

In this powerful verse, Paul uses spiritual eyes to see things that we often miss with our natural perspective. Believers are the representation of Jesus on earth through the Holy Spirit in them. If you want your kids to know Jesus, helping them to know other solid believers is a place to start.

In the last chapter we saw that Jesus is the greatest representation of God Himself, but Jesus has gone away and left His Holy Spirit in us so that we can represent Him. Are you surrounding your children with people who are representing the very nature of God? Who is reflecting Jesus to your kids? A mosaic is made up of many pieces, so your life and that of your children is made up by the relationships that surround it.

Worship and Pancakes

One of the young women I respect as much as anyone I know is our church's worship leader Beejay. Apart from my wife, she is a role model I want my daughters to grow up to emulate. She is honest, kind, funky and loves Jesus passionately. Next week, she and my daughter will have breakfast together. At 7:00 AM on Tuesday, I will be dropping Lily off at the local pancake house with a $20 bill. An hour later, I am going to come back and take her to school. First of all, we thank God that we have someone like Beejay who is willing to get up so early to have pancakes with a seven-year-old.

We are excited to see how Beejay and Lily will rub off on each other. We are also stoked to have another voice in the choir of Lily's life. As a former youth pastor, I know how crucial these relationships are. I can't tell you how many secrets kids confided in me when they didn't feel comfortable telling their parents. From big mistakes to advice on how to deal with a friend who was caught up in drugs, Karie and I were able to be there when some kids felt their parents could not.

I'd like to think that Lily and Lucy will always be able to share anything with us, but I know better. I am not the solution to all of their problems, nor do I have all the answers. Because of this, Karie and I make it a point to have other people like Beejay on the family camping trip we call life.

A parenting team is a group of people you surround your family with. These are the people who have a say in your life. They know you and your children better than anyone else. They are the kind of people you give permission to speak into your life. They are people who are committed to you and your family, and you are committed to theirs.

This does not only have to be other parents. Your team can range from coaches to youth leaders in your church and even to godly neighbors. While not all of these people will have the same level of influence or importance, all will be another brick in the solid foundation you are laying for your kids' lives.

The Counsel of the Council

In the book of Proverbs, we see that victory and success come through the counsel of many advisors. The same is true for your kids. You most definitely do not want their only perspective on life and faith to be yours. There is strength in numbers, and the more examples they have of people who are living boldly for God, the stronger their own faith will become.

> For lack of guidance a nation falls, but many advisers make victory sure (Prov. 11:14).

> Plans fail for lack of counsel, but with many advisers they succeed (Prov. 15:22).

> For waging war you need guidance, and for victory many advisers (Prov. 24:6).

One of the best examples I have seen of this is from our friends Doug and Kristen. They are committed to partnering with people who are quality examples and in relationships that their teenagers can count on and lean on if necessary.

An instance of this is when their son, Peyton, turned 13. As a messianic Jew (Doug), this was a significant birthday and one Doug and Kristen wanted to impress upon their son.

On the night of his son's birthday, Doug took Peyton down to the beach. On the sand that night were a group of men whom Doug and Kristen had made it a point to surround their son with. These were men who had been part of family camping trips, Sunday Charger football game BBQs and the general fabric of their life.

After praying with his son, Doug sent Peyton to walk down the beach. About every hundred yards stood one of the men who had made a difference in Peyton's life. Each was holding a flashlight, and each time Doug's son came to another one of the figures holding a light, he would be welcomed, given some advice for the journey into manhood and prayed over. Peyton walked the beach savoring the moment until he came to the next member of the council. At the end of the journey, all the men gathered around to pray a blessing and ask God for anointing on Peyton's life.

Doug gave his son an opportunity to walk with Jesus on a beach that night in the form of believing men who were and are being transformed into the very image of Jesus!

I realize this type of event might be a long way from where you are right now. I am not proposing that you need to re-create it. What I want to do is encourage you to make a dedicated effort to cultivate quality relationships for your kids.

Send your kid to the zoo with a family that has the aroma of Jesus on them. Let him or her volunteer as an usher at church under the supervision of a Spirit-led usher. Set up a time for ice cream with your kids and the lead pastor. Get a quality young woman from your college group to be a nanny one day a week. Who cares if you don't need a nanny; it will bless the young woman you are employing and bring more of Jesus into your home!

Their Voices and Our Purpose

If you have been a believer for any amount of time, you have probably found direction for your life in the counsel of believing friends. Often, others see in us what we cannot see in ourselves. Having committed believers around your children will help them find their identity and purpose. Here is an example of what I mean.

When I was 12, I used a particularly savory and foul four-letter word to let my mom know how I was really feeling. Unfortunately, I used it on a day that I was supposed to be the starting pitcher for my Little League team. I ended up missing the game that day and being banished to the car to sit until we were ready to leave the event we were at.

What I did not know as I walked out to the car was that God was getting ready to speak to me. God would, that day, tell me for the first time that I was going to be a pastor.

As I sat and fumed in the back of the car, up came Lloyd. Lloyd and his wife, Betty, were good friends of the family and incredible grandparent-like figures in my life. Lloyd had paid attention to me as a kid, taken me out to play catch and swatted the ping-pong ball with me more than I could remember. At that point, Lloyd was the only person I would even listen to in the midst of a frenzy of tears and protest. He had won the right to be heard.

Lloyd opened the door and began to talk to me about life, God and baseball. While I don't remember all that he said that day, I do remember one thing clearly. Lloyd said that one day I would bless God with my mouth and I might even be a preacher. He was right!

Long before my parents knew that I would be called to full-time pastoral ministry, one of the men of God in my life saw something of the future in me and was able to share it in a way that I never forgot. This was the first time I ever heard this vision for my future, but it ended up being one of the countless times that people have affirmed God's call on my life.

I could mention dozens of other people that God has used to communicate His message of love for me. At many crucial times, especially when I was a kid, Jesus was there in the form of believers who were being transformed into His image. It was as if I was speaking to Jesus Himself. In a way, I was.

The Bad Apples

Now lets talk about those "bad apples." I believe in the potential of bad apples. The reason I do is that I was one. The problem with being a bad apple was that none of the good apples wanted to hang out with me. I was the pariah of the youth group, and eventually I was asked not to come back.

I wonder what would have happened if some of the "good" kids had asked me to hang out with them a few times? What if some of them had reached out? Instead, there was a huge separation between "us" and "them," the smokers and the stiffs. Heck, I even remember some parent meetings where I was the main topic. The word got around. Keep your kids away from Adam!

I guess you can see where I am going with this. While you most definitely want to surround your kids with the people of God, I want to challenge you to work with your kids to reach out to some of the fringe kids—kids who don't have the best home life or opportunities.

You and your child know who these kids are. They are not hard to spot. What if you worked with your child to reach out to some of these kids? What if you and your son decided to invite one of these children on the family campout along with your son's other friends? The key is that there is safety in numbers. As long as you are wise and aware, this is a great way to teach your child to not only be a witness, but also to be a loving friend to a child who needs it.

If you do this in prayer and through the direction of the Holy Spirit, you will not only be igniting the fire of God in your child's social life, but maybe in the life of another family who needs the transforming power of Jesus in their lives!

Getting There (Part One)

Make plans this week to put Jesus into your week in the form of other believers. Plan a play date, park or beach day. Have a BBQ at your house. Bring together the people of God and hang out together. Let them increase the aroma of Jesus in the lives of your children (see 2 Cor. 2:14-16).

Teach your kids to seek wisdom from the council. The next time your child has a difficult decision or question, seek out a person you and your child are comfortable with and send them out together for ice cream. Tell your kid that you want a report as to their perspective and advice. In this way you will be teaching your kids to seek wisdom from other godly people.

Reach out to a bad apple. He or she is not bad anyway, just overripe!

Getting There (Part Two)

Develop a small-group community. While I try not to be dogmatic, on this point I am. You need to be in a small group. Don't wait for your church to initiate a small-group program before you take advantage of Jesus in your midst in the form of other Christians. Step out and start your own. Find a group with whom you feel you can connect and start a weekly gathering at one of the homes.

Seek God in this process and ask Him to lay certain individuals on your heart. Pay particular attention to their children. Is there godly direction and discipline in the home? Are these the kind of kids you would want your children to be with on a regular basis? Do you see things in their kids that you want to rub off on yours?

Remember, the people you are surrounded with most often are who you are becoming.

For Karie and me, our small group is essential. We've been meeting together for five years, and we've had our ups and downs. In those five years an important thing that has developed is that we have a group of people to support and pray for us in the rhythms of our life and vice versa.

This consistent and stable Christ-centered weekly event has become a landmark in our lives. In a small-group environment Christ can come alive to your kids on a regular basis. This is what is called raising children in community. So put the book down right now, pick up your phone, and initiate a small group with other Christian parents you know and respect.

Thanks, Lloyd

While writing this book, I got the news that Lloyd had only a few weeks to live. His cancer had flared up again. I immediately got on the phone and talked to him and Betty, one last time. A couple of weeks later, he passed away.

You have to understand that these people prayed for me on their knees every night for more than 28 years. This is not a pastor's exaggeration; it was *literally* every night for 28 years. Lloyd and Betty are old school. I believe that if they had not been on my mom's parenting team, I would not be alive today. Their prayers went to war against the schemes of the devil.

The last time we talked, I shared with Lloyd what he meant to me and how God had used him as a prophetic voice in my life. It seems that I caught him at a low point when the devil was trying to convince him that his life had been a waste. We wept and talked about everything from ping-pong to the glory of Jesus. I said good-bye, knowing that we would not speak again in this life. Still, we were both left with a sense of the joy of Jesus.

Today, Lloyd lives deep in my heart. The lessons he taught and the life he lived have penetrated me to the core, spilling over into the way I shepherd my girls. Whenever I preach, his voice echoes in the words.

Give Your Kids the Keys:

Teaching Kids to Live According to the Spirit

Coveting
by Lily Stadtmiller

One day, my friend brought animal pencil toppers called squishers to school. After that, almost all of the class had some. I also got some, but whenever I play with the squishers I don't think about God. It is like I am hypnotized. It sometimes feels like they are more important then God. That is not good.

CHAPTER 9

Digging for God

*Realize what you really want. It stops you from chasing butterflies
and puts you to work digging gold.*
WILLIAM MARSTON[1]

There is a dinosaur fossil excavation exhibit at Legoland, in Carlsbad, California. Whenever we visit the park, our kids make a beeline for the "dig" area. There, they can search for cement bones buried beneath the surface of a giant sandbox. For a few bucks you can rent some digging tools, shovels, brushes, and so on.

At first, we can't tell what we're digging up; but after a little while, we're able to distinguish what we've found. Sometimes it is a T-rex. Other times it is a pterodactyl. It doesn't really matter what it ends up being. The cool part is that we discovered it together and there is an excitement not only in the discovery, but also in the search.

Now imagine that instead of allowing my children to dig for bones with me, I took them to the exhibit and let them see what I found earlier in the day. Sure, they would be interested. These are dinosaur bones, after all; but would they have the same interest, excitement and understanding as they would from being on the dig with me? Would they know there were tools available for them to dig? Would they even know they were allowed into the giant sandbox?

Seeking after God involves the system that archaeologists use. It is a four-step process—surveying, excavation, data collection and analysis—that helps them understand our past and find clues to our future.

In this chapter, I want to help you take your kids on a dig of their own. This is your chance to be Indiana Jones. This time, instead of searching for the "holy grail," the longed-for treasure is God Himself.

They Can't Dig if You're Always Holding the Shovel

Parents are one of the biggest challenges kids face in regard to seeking after the will of God. I say this because I have not experienced many parents who actively encourage their children to figure out what God is saying to them individually. This is like telling your kids to dig but never giving them the shovel.

Children need to be given an opportunity to seek God on their own. Parents often give their children truth but fail at letting them be truth seekers. The difference is fundamentally crucial.

I understand why we do this as parents. It comes from a place of wanting to point children toward right living. The problem is that, once again, we are training our children to be dependent on our faith for their lives.

Ten Bucks Goes a Long Way in Mexico

When Lily was five years old, Karie and I decided it was time to take her on a home build in Mexico. It is a life-changing experience for everyone involved. Within a period of 10 hours, a family goes from having no shelter to moving into a small three-room home with a loft.

I believe that the best way for your children to learn gratitude and compassion for the less fortunate is to let them experience it. Some time spent in the slums of a third-world country or impoverished area in our own country will teach your children a lot more than telling them about all the starving children in Africa. Don't get me wrong, you should do that as well; but putting skin on the stories really makes an impact.

On the night before we left, Lily wanted me to help count the money in her piggy bank. She had roughly $10. At this point, Lily didn't know much about money, so it held little value to her. I asked her what she wanted to do with her 10 bucks. She shrugged her shoulders.

The next thing I did is something I encourage you to do. I asked her what she thought God wanted her to do with it. She said she had no idea, and she asked me what I thought. I told her that I had no idea, that it was her money and that it was up to her to determine how to use it. I did tell her that God had a purpose for that particular $10 in the same way that He has a purpose for every resource He blesses us with.

I encouraged her to go into her room and sit in her rocking chair for three minutes to listen for God speaking to her heart. I told her that God will often give us a thought through the Holy Spirit if we are willing to slow down and listen.

Curious, Lily headed off to her room. I had no idea what might happen. When she came out she said that she thought she had heard God say that He wanted her to give the money to someone in Mexico the next day. As a parent, I was excited about this decision, but I also knew that the money had no value to her. I decided to up the ante.

"Okay, Lily, that sounds like it might be God, but did you know that your 10 bucks is enough to get you a Webkinz?" This occurred during a Webkinz craze in our community. I think Lily would have traded her sister for one of those plush dolls.

I saw a look come over her face that said, "Oh no, what have I done? This can't be happening." She then told me that she thought maybe God had not told her to give the money away. I told her that she might be right and that it is always good to test everything we think we hear from God.

Test everything. Hold on to the good (1 Thess. 5:21).

I suggested that she give God another listen and that I would support whatever she felt she heard. With a pained expression, Lily went back into her room. This time she was in there a bit longer. Eventually the door opened, she came out and handed me the $10. "I want to give it away, Daddy. I think that God wants me to give it away."

While I was filled with joy at this selfless act, I did not want to get so excited that she might begin to find her reward in my response to these movements of God in her life.

"Well, Lily," I said, "you might be right. That sounds like something that God might say, but why are you handing the money to me?" Lily replied that she wanted me to give it to the people for her. To this I replied, "It's not my money. You are going to have to ask God who He wants you to give it to."

"How will I know that, Daddy?" she asked. As before, I assured her that God would show her. She just needed to listen to her heart and to the Lord the next day. I am a firm believer that it is very difficult to miss God's will, especially if you are looking for it. I believed that if she was meant to give the money away, she would know. I figure if God wants you to do something, He will make it clear. He is God, after all.

Lily—with a tattered $10 bill and a purpose—and I, with my cup of coffee, hit the road at 4:30 A.M. the next day. By 6:00 A.M., we had crossed the border. By 7:00 A.M., the sound of the pounding of nails was ringing through the neighborhood of shanty houses and open sewers.

Lily was a champion that day. She painted in the sun for two hours straight, worked the nail gun with me and installed windows. About every hour Lily would ask me about a certain person she had seen. "Do you think that is who I should give the money to?" Each time we would talk it out, and each time the decision was hers.

By 5:00 P.M., it was time to pack up, and Lily had found no one that she felt God was telling her to give the money to. I was starting to pray at this point. While I know that God never lets us down, I still worried that this might end up as a lesson on how not to hear from God. It wasn't what I had hoped for.

We waited an hour in line at the border, and it was time to cross back in to the US. We were three cars away from crossing when Lily asked me about the money again. I told her that God had a purpose for the money. I have to confess that I was beginning to wonder if it was true.

At that moment, seemingly out of nowhere, a disheveled woman carrying a baby walked up and knocked on Lily's window. If you have done the border wait drill, then you know this is extremely rare; not because there are a lack of people asking for help, but because the woman chose to go to the window of a five-year-old, rather than an adult. Kindergarteners are not known for being flush with cash.

> Don't let your desire to train your kids in the way of the Lord get in the way of teaching them how to find God on their own.

Lily rolled down the window and the two stared at each other for what seemed like an eternity. The woman said only one word, "Please." In the mirror behind me, I could see Lily clutching the bill in her hand. She had been holding it the entire hour in line, waiting for God to speak. Lily reached up and opened her hand, giving her money and potential Webkinz away. As we drove away, the woman called out, "*Valle con Dios*," or "Go with God." I can assure you that we did!

I don't tell you this story to highlight my daughter's benevolence. I tell it to challenge you to begin believing in your kids' ability to seek and hear from God. What I mean is, get out of the way! Don't let your desire to train them in the way of the Lord get in the way of teaching them how to find God on their own.

A Boy Named Samuel and the Word of the Lord

There are many stories in the Bible to look at for parenting cues. When it comes to seeking and hearing the voice of God, the account of Samuel as a boy is one of the most encouraging. In it we see God speaking to a child about the path of an entire nation.

The boy Samuel ministered before the LORD under Eli. In those days the word of the LORD was rare; there were not many visions. One night Eli, whose eyes were becoming so weak that he could barely see, was lying down in his usual place. The lamp of God had not yet gone out, and Samuel was lying down in the temple of the LORD, where the ark of God was. Then the LORD called Samuel.

Samuel answered, "Here I am." And he ran to Eli and said, "Here I am; you called me."

But Eli said, "I did not call; go back and lie down." So he went and lay down. Again the LORD called, "Samuel!" And Samuel got up and went to Eli and said, "Here I am; you called me."

"My son," Eli said, "I did not call; go back and lie down."

Now Samuel did not yet know the LORD: The word of the LORD had not yet been revealed to him. The LORD called Samuel a third time, and Samuel got up and went to Eli and said, "Here I am; you called me."

Then Eli realized that the LORD was calling the boy. So Eli told Samuel, "Go and lie down, and if he calls you, say, 'Speak, LORD, for your servant is listening.'" So Samuel went and lay down in his place.

The LORD came and stood there, calling as at the other times, "Samuel! Samuel!"

Then Samuel said, "Speak, for your servant is listening." And the LORD said to Samuel: "See, I am about to do something in Israel that will make the ears of everyone who hears of it tingle. . . ."

Samuel lay down until morning and then opened the doors of the house of the LORD. He was afraid to tell Eli the vision, but Eli called him and said, "Samuel, my son."

Samuel answered, "Here I am."

"What was it he said to you?" Eli asked. "Do not hide it from me. May God deal with you, be it ever so severely, if you hide from me anything he told you." So Samuel told him everything, hiding nothing from him. Then Eli said, "He is the LORD; let him do what is good in his eyes."

The LORD was with Samuel as he grew up, and he let none of his words fall to the ground. And all Israel from Dan to Beersheba recognized that Samuel was attested as a prophet of the LORD. The LORD continued to appear at Shiloh, and there he revealed himself to Samuel through his word (1 Sam. 3:1-11,15-21).

Eli was not a role model to emulate on a regular basis, but in this instance he was spot-on. The first interesting thing I see in this story is that Eli took on the role of father figure to Samuel. Perhaps the error of his ways with his two sons, Hophni and Phinehas, caused him to desire another chance at doing it right. Maybe it was just custom. Regardless, the story illustrates a way of parenting that is worth paying attention to.

Survey, Excavate, Collect and Analyze

Eli guides Samuel in the pattern of all great archaeologists. First, Samuel is encouraged to survey the situation by going in and waiting on God to speak. Next he is told to dig in (excavate) and inquire about what the Lord wants to say. Finally, Samuel is asked to collect the data and report it to Eli for analysis.

Survey

Eli had been a priest for many years. He had heard the voice of God before and he knew that it often came during moments of stillness. He encouraged Samuel to go, lie down and listen. The habit of listening is difficult, but it is an important thing to encourage your children to develop. Kids who aren't taught to listen are kids who have nothing to say. The same is true for parents.

Something my mom always says to Lily and Lucy is that attention is a commodity; it needs to be paid out. That is why we "pay" attention. Listening takes effort. The payoff for listening is that we can gain something that changes us. It brings a new level of understanding.

Another payoff for listening is "knowing." When God speaks, we learn and grow in wisdom, knowledge and understanding. This is valuable compensation. When we begin feeling that God is speaking to us, we gain a hunger for more of His voice. We become more interested in paying attention.

As a pastor, I want to be consistent in listening to what God is communicating to me. As a believer, and especially as a believing parent, it is imperative that I listen for what God is saying to me.

The Bible reigns supreme as God's primary tool of communication, but I have experienced that God also speaks in additional ways. He regularly speaks to me through my thoughts, the counsel of other believers, His creation, music, commercials, movies and through my kids.

While I don't always get it right, I have learned to know His voice. God promises this in His Word. In John 10:4 Jesus tells His disciples that sheep will know His voice. This is a great metaphor to share with your kids. Tell them that they are sheep and that God is their Shepherd. This will most likely aid in their times of listening (prayer).

> When he has brought out all his own, he goes on ahead of them, and his sheep follow him because they know his voice (John 10:4).

Once you have learned to hear the Shepherd's voice, you will want to put your findings to the test. Before we get to that, we need to take a quick look at learning to recognize His voice.

I have learned to know the voice of God by paying attention to what I call the "sweater of my soul." Let me explain. Have you ever bought a new sweater? If you have, you know how annoying it is when you snag it on a nail or some other sharp object. Immediately, a little loop is pulled out that is fully visible, no matter how small.

The voice of God works the same way. When I'm reading the Word, listening to worship music or watching a commercial, God will sometimes pull on the sweater of my soul. Something will stick out to me and I develop a keener awareness.

Teaching your children to hear God's voice is about helping them to become aware. The voice of God, simply put, is God making you aware of something. If I become aware of something that seems like it might be from God, I assume that it is. This could be to speak a word of encouragement to someone who is downcast or meet the immediate need of a homeless couple asking for assistance. Either way, I begin by assuming this is God speaking. There is no sin in believing that God is speaking. The problem comes when we don't test what we think we have heard. Once again, assuming that something is from God does not mean that you act on it right away. It just means that you begin testing what you think you heard. Not doing this is why many feel they never hear from God.

In the story of Samuel, we see that the young boy's "sweater" got caught. He did not initially know that it was God calling him, but he was made aware of something unique. Something stuck out.

I want you to start asking your kids about what is tugging on their heart sweaters. Tomorrow morning, challenge them to listen for God all day. Assure them that God speaks to His sheep. He is God; if He wants to speak, He will. One thing I will assure you of is this: If you read God's Word to them in the morning before they leave for school or begin their day, their sweater is more likely to get pulled.

We try to have a snack time when Lily gets home from school. It's an environment she looks forward to and it helps her little heart to be more geared toward response. After you are well into cookie time, remind your child about the challenge. Ask what he or she might have thought God said to them during the day. What caught their attention?

Excavate

I have a feeling that you are going to be surprised by this experiment. Even if your child has no idea of what God might have said, it is a moment for analysis. Begin to inquire into what happened that day. What did your child find on the dig site?

We see that the priest Eli did this when he questioned Samuel as to what he had heard. In this way, Samuel was made responsible for his own faith. Even though Eli guided young Samuel, it was up to Samuel to find God on his own. Your job as a parent is to help analyze the data your child brings back from the dig.

Being able to ask questions and attain meaningful answers and possible solutions from a child is an art form. I find it funny that kids will ask a limitless number of questions and then clam up as soon as you begin to question them.

In my relationship with Lily, this happens for a number of reasons. One is when she senses that I am trying to lead her to an answer that I think is correct rather than listening to her heart. Another barrier is my inability to become a seven-year-old in my approach to drawing her out. Karie and I have found that Lily responds best when she feels that we respect her ability to hear from God.

Eli valued Samuel's ability to hear and communicate the message of God, even though Samuel was only a young child. I see this as one of the most important components in teaching your children to hear from the Father. If you do not respect their spiritual ability the way God does, they will know it. Not only that, but your lack of trust might cause them to question the times when God really is speaking to them.

I believe that less than 5 percent of believing children are able to assimilate, process and respond to God's voice. I don't believe that God is not speaking to them, just that they have not been shepherded in this arena. If I had to put my finger on the key reason why so many teens leave the church after graduation, it would be this one fact. They don't know God's voice, so they don't really know God. After all, how do you follow a God you don't know?

Collect the Data and Analyze
A key to making good decisions is having all of the information in front of you before you act. You don't want to jump in and start making conclusions and assumptions as your child shares what he

or she thinks God is speaking. Even if your child says something that is biblically inaccurate like, "God told me to punch Billy in the nose," you still want to take it all in first. Remember, the process of hearing from God is just that, a process. Don't get ahead of yourself or your child.

Finally, after you get all of the data out on the table, it is time to clean and assemble the bones. This is the fun part, and we will discuss this process a bit later.

Getting There

Something that God has made Karie and me aware of lately is that we make too many family plans without His guidance or our kids' involvement. This is why this year we have decided not to take our summer vacation until we've decided together where God would have us go.

This week, apply this chapter to a family decision and let your kids seek God's heart on the matter. If you have not planned your vacation yet, this might be a good place to start.

A fun way to do this is to pull out a map or use the Internet to begin to dig. Write down anything that any of you hear in the journal you created.

Pray that God would give your family unity in the decision. Unity is a primary way to test God's voice. In the end, you as a parent have the responsibility to make decisions for your family, but you can rarely go wrong by bringing your children into this process as often as possible.

Note
1. While I realize that William Marston is not a terrific example to be followed in his personal life decisions, I still found this quote to be worthy of repeating.

The Voice of God

The Bible does not provide a map for life, only a compass.
HADDON ROBINSON

The Holy Spirit Is Your Personal GPS

If you want to explain the voice of God to your kids, I suggest you test-drive a new car with GPS (Global Positioning System). Maybe you have seen one of these. They are so cool. As you drive around, a voice speaks to you from a digital map on the dashboard. Type in where you want to go and the little voice in the dashboard will guide you there: "Stop, go straight, turn right at the next exit . . . you look amazing today." Okay, it does not say that. I love that you can program the GPS in cool voices to guide you along the way. If you want directions from a British professor or a New York taxi driver, they are all available to you.

The Holy Spirit is your own personal GPS system and the very voice of God within you. There are three similarities to the voice of God and a GPS system. Teach all of these to your child:

1. You expect the GPS to speak to you; you should expect the same from God.

2. In the same way that you can program a voice into the GPS, God has also programmed you to hear Him in a voice that is unique to you.

3. Global Positioning Systems are programmed with all of the answers you need to get you where you want to go. Because you have the presence of God within you, you already have access to every answer you will ever need. By using God's Word as a guide, the Holy Spirit's voice will lead the way.

Before we move on, I want to highlight that the voice of God is different from the Word of God. The voice of God is the Holy Spirit's guidance within you. The Holy Spirit is your internal compass and guide. He brings meaning and understanding to things, such as God's written Word; dangerous situations where you should show caution; conviction of sin; and if you should stop to help a person in need. To be sure, God's voice is found within His Word, but I am using "voice" here to represent the guidance of the Holy Spirit, which transmits the Word to our hearts.

Expect Your External GPS to Speak

In the Scriptures below, you will see that the Holy Spirit is a teacher who directs us from within.

Whenever you are arrested and brought to trial, do not worry beforehand about what to say. Just say whatever is given you at the time, for it is not you speaking, but the Holy Spirit (Mark 13:11).

The Holy Spirit will teach you at that time what you should say (Luke 12:12).

It had been revealed to him by the Holy Spirit that he would not die before he had seen the Lord's Christ (Luke 2:26).

But the Counselor, the Holy Spirit, whom the Father will send in my name, will teach you all things and will remind you of everything I have said to you (John 14:26).

In each of these verses the Holy Spirit is seen as a teacher who makes sure that His message is clear to those who are looking for it. This is a great analogy your children can understand easily. Tell them that the Holy Spirit is a teacher whose classroom is their heart.

As I've already said, I haven't seen many parents who treat their children like they can hear from God on their own. If you are one of these parents, I suggest that you start expecting God to speak to your children.

Since God is in the business of talking to His children (anyone who has called upon Jesus as Savior and Lord), I try to assume that He is speaking to us. We have tried to raise our children to expect the same. This is not a difficult environment to create. You begin by just regularly asking your kids, "What is God saying to you about that?"

For instance, if your daughter is struggling because her soccer coach is not putting her in the game and she complains about it to you, ask her what God is saying to her about it. When your five-year-old son is angry with a classmate, ask the same. Heck, why not ask your two-year-old? Is this not how you taught them to speak and understand language? Every word they now understand started out as a word they didn't understand. What you are affirming to them is that you believe that God speaks!

Karie and I tell our girls that whenever they become aware of a thought or emotion that crosses their soul or mind and seems to have the scent of God on it, assume that God is speaking. This does not mean that we encourage them to immediately move into the action mode, or that they got it right; but it does insert an awareness of God into the situation.

Lucy Smells God

When working with my two-year-old, Lucy, in learning how to become aware of God's voice, I have started using the analogy of flowers. Last week, Karie had the flu and I got to be Mr. Mom for two days. It was fantastic. I'm a pattern guy, so both of those days followed a similar routine. About noon each day, Lucy and I would head out on the road for our walk. On the first day, we came across a neighbor's rose garden. We had a great time smelling the roses, looking at the thorns, and so on. It was fantastical.

While we were there, the Holy Spirit reminded me of 2 Corinthians 2:15. I told Lucy that God made the rose to have a pretty smell. I then told her that if we have Jesus in our hearts, we also have a pretty smell when we are nice.

> For we are to God the aroma of Christ among those who are being saved and those who are perishing (2 Cor. 2:15).

I told her that God has a fragrant aroma and that it is our job to smell God. While I am sure this might have been a little deep for her, she got it later that day when she shared a cookie with her sister. Right there, when that happened, I said, "Hey, Lucy, that was really nice; you smell like God right now."

In ways like this, Karie and I are trying to teach our children what God's voice and actions sound and look like. We are trying to make it simple, easy and practical. We have tried to use the conversations that surround the story of our life to disciple our kids.

By the way, this is not a new and revolutionary technique. It was the way Jesus discipled. He did it on the move. He did it with random conversations and analogies that made sense.

Through a simple analogy of a flower or some other tangible example the Holy Spirit gives you, you will be able to communicate with your two-year-old about how to see and hear from God.

With Lucy, all I need to ask when she is faced with a decision is, "What decision smells like God?" While she might not always know the answer, it once again allows us to have a conversation about the story of our life and how we join God's story. It also puts Lucy in charge of her own hearing. God gave her ears for a reason. If God wanted us as parents to hear for our children, He would have put their ears on our heads. Since He did not do that, I am assuming that it is a better model as a parent to teach them to be hearers.

Teach your kids to expect to hear from God! As long as you put a good testing plan in place, your children will come to know a God who directs their paths (see Ps. 23:3).

Check Out Your Expectations

I can almost hear someone saying, "Whoa, slow down, Adam! I don't think we should be making such bold statements and setting our kids up for failure when they don't hear from God regularly." Okay, you might be right; but if that is what you are thinking, let's compare your same expectation to the natural realm of your children's development.

If you think about your child's ability to process voice in the natural world, you would expect most children to begin understanding language before they are even a year old. If your child is not communicating well by the middle of his or her second year, you would assume there is a problem. Most children can understand a language, or even two languages, by this age.

At this same age, we also assume that a child can not only understand a language but also respond appropriately. The question I want to ask is, why don't we have the same expectation when it comes to a child's ability to hear in the spiritual realm, which, for a Christian, is just as real as what we perceive with our natural senses (even more so)?

I believe that children actually begin to learn, process and understand the voice of God long before they even know the voice of their parent. We see this happening in the life of John the Baptist, who heard from the Holy Spirit as a fetus and leapt in the womb of Elizabeth his mother.

> When Elizabeth heard Mary's greeting, the baby leaped in her womb, and Elizabeth was filled with the Holy Spirit (Luke 1:41).

Once again, the point is whether you have more faith in the natural abilities of your child than in their spiritual abilities.

Believe in Your Child's Ability to Hear from God

In the late nineties, when I was working with Young Life, I had the great privilege of being a part of an outreach to special-needs students at Dana Hills High School in Dana Point, California. The class I was a part of had students with a wide range of challenges, from very functional to nearly vegetative.

One thing I learned from that experience was that each of these children of God had the ability to experience God. Over and over I watched as God was able to break down what I perceived as an insurmountable barrier and reach these kids. I saw kids who rarely responded come alive when I would bring my guitar and play worship songs. The God of the universe is not limited by a person's disabilities.

I have had the same experience praying for people in comas. I have watched people move when prayed over, even though they had not moved in days. On two occasions, heart monitors that beat at a slow and steady pace for hours began to race when I prayed with them.

Your children are spiritual giants and have a massive ability for a deep relationship with God.

Remember from the verses on page 121 that God is the teacher. He knows how to teach each of His students individually. Your child is getting personal tutoring from the Holy Spirit Himself. There are no overcrowded classrooms in the school of the Holy Spirit. They will not get lost in the shuffle. Having this view of your children will change the way you parent.

If you begin to respect your children's spiritual ability to hear from and process the voice and or leadings of God, you will begin to give them more opportunities to experience God, regardless of their age. I know that it has for us.

The First Story They Ever Heard

Lily and Lucy had very different birthing experiences, but both experienced one thing in common. The first story they ever heard was the story of God's love for mankind. Karie and I believed that even at one hour old, Lily and Lucy could process God's story in a way that we could not comprehend, because we serve a supernatural God!

On the day of each girl's birth, she was surrounded by family and friends. You would have thought we had hired a film and camera crew both times; it was a bit chaotic. We did all the mandatory pictures, and all the grandparents and close relatives got to meet the new addition. By the time that was all over, we were ready to be alone with our little bundle.

Eventually, everyone left and we were in our hospital room. It was just the three of us. After Karie got her cuddle and bonding time in, I took our baby into my arms. It was story time.

I said, "In the beginning, a God who loves you created the heavens and the earth." Over the next few minutes I spoke over my little girl the greatest story ever told. I shared about the God who loved her and about the Son of God who had given up everything so that He might rescue her from the biggest mistake ever made. I shared with her the gospel of Jesus Christ.

Do I believe my baby understood what I shared at that time? Yes, I do. In her inner being she got it. Here's what God says about it:

> For the word of God is living and active. Sharper than any double-edged sword, it penetrates even to dividing soul and spirit, joints and marrow; it judges the thoughts and attitudes of the heart (Heb. 4:12).

> As the rain and the snow come down from heaven . . . so is my word that goes out from my mouth: It will not return to me empty, but will accomplish what I desire and achieve the purpose for which I sent it (Isa. 55:10-11).

I believe this not only because I have experienced it before but also because I believe our eternal spiritual ability and God's power are far greater then our ability in the natural. I believe that the gospel holds the power of God, and this event right after birth set

in motion a life in Christ for both of our children. It set a seal upon
their hearts.

What You Affirm

When Jesus became aware of Peter hearing from God, He let him
know about it. He encouraged Peter in the fact that he could hear
from the Holy Spirit.

> Simon Peter answered, "You are the Christ, the Son of the
> living God." Jesus replied, "Blessed are you, Simon son of
> Jonah, for this was not revealed to you by man, but by my
> Father in heaven" (Matt. 16:16-17).

Let your children know when they say or do things that have
the mark of Christ on them. Jesus told Peter that the Holy Spirit
was speaking to him. He affirms Peter in his hearing. While I am
not sure how Peter got the message that day, as the Word does not
tell us, you can be sure the next time he got the same sort of message, he would be a lot more apt to understand that it was from
God. This is the exact model you want to follow when you hear or
see your kids doing things that have the mark of Christ on them.

Their Own Personal Voice

Because we are all unique, we will hear the voice of God in different ways. The truth of God's message will never change, but when
He speaks, God does respect the uniqueness of how He created
each of us. Karie hears God in a small voice that communicates
words to her mind. Other times she has dreams and prays for God
to reveal their meaning through His Word or another avenue.

I see pictures and images in my mind, as I am a visionary
thinker. Once, during a prayer time, when I was asking God how
I should treat my wife, I immediately saw a picture of Karie as a
queen dressed in shining white. What I took from that was that
God wants me to treat her with respect, honor and purity. Other
times, I get struck by deep emotion or conviction.

How do you hear from God? When was the last time you felt a prompting from the Holy Spirit? What about your kids? When was the last time they heard from God, or thought they did? Have you questioned them about how they came to that understanding? Have you affirmed them recently in their hearing? Do they even know that God is speaking to them when He does, or like Peter, are they waiting for you to play the role of Jesus and begin to disciple them in the way of knowing God?

Like Jesus with Peter, affirm the times that they feel they have heard from God. Ask them how they came up with that impression or thought. Were there emotions attached to it? Were they reminded of a Bible verse? Here again, you are teaching your kids to be aware and active in their faith.

The Answer Is Already There

In the same way that a GPS has all of the information it needs to guide you in the right path, you are already filled with every answer or solution to the life you are living.

Here is how it breaks down theologically. If God dwells within you and is all-knowing, then you have access to all the knowledge of God that you need to know to follow His purposes. I am not saying that you are all-knowing. If you were all-knowing, then you would be omniscient. That is a character trait that is unique to God.

This is an important distinction when teaching your children to know God for themselves. Think about the GPS again. If you have a GPS, all of the answers are there. You only need to pay attention to the voice in the dashboard to know where to go. If you don't have a GPS, you will need to stop and ask directions on a regular basis. Each person you ask might have the right directions and point you to the correct path, but then again, they might not.

When discipling your kids to follow God, you will want to assure them that while they do look outside themselves to collect data or excavate, in the end the final decision comes from being in tune with the little voice within their hearts and its alignment with the truth of God's Word.

In the next several verses, the Bible confirms the internal GPS metaphor.

> The knowledge of the secrets of the kingdom of God has been given to you, but to others I speak in parables, so that, "though seeing, they may not see; though hearing, they may not understand" (Luke 8:10).

> My purpose is that they may be encouraged in heart and united in love . . . in order that they may know the mystery of God, namely, Christ, in whom are hidden all the treasures of wisdom and knowledge (Col. 2:2-3).

> His divine power has given us everything we need for life and godliness through our knowledge of him who called us by his own glory and goodness (2 Pet. 1:3).

This is important for all believers to understand. Knowing this changes the model of looking outside of ourselves for God's direction to one that is internally based. It affirms that finding the direction for right living is based in knowing Jesus first and then getting direction from the Holy Spirit. God's voice and direction always come as a result of knowing Him intimately. Thus, when you teach your kids to seek or listen in order to hear God, make sure they are seeking a relationship with Jesus, rather than an answer to their problem.

Where to Start

Please don't hear me saying some New Age philosophy that tells you to seek within, or that if you teach your child to empty himself and look within, he will find inner light, peace and direction.

What I am saying is that everything you need is found in Christ, and every search begins with Christ. Let me explain it in parenting terms. Imagine that you and your spouse have decided to increase your family through adoption. The place to begin that enquiry is by focusing on Jesus. Before you check out adoption websites, or pray for direction about the matter at hand or seek counsel from your pastor or friends, you will want to begin by fixing your eyes on Jesus.

This could be done in worship, by reading the Word or just by meditating on Jesus through the Scriptures. The point is that because all answers are in Him, that is where you start.

> Let us fix our eyes on Jesus, the author and perfecter of our faith, who for the joy set before him endured the cross, scorning its shame, and sat down at the right hand of the throne of God (Heb. 12:2).

I love this verse because it once again speaks of story. God is a perfect author who is writing the story of your life. The way to walk into that story is not by questioning the plot on a regular basis, but rather to put Him first; to let Him know that He is what you are seeking and everything else is secondary. As believers, we know that if we employ this principle we can't go wrong in regard to hearing from Him or being led in the right direction.

> But seek his kingdom, and these things will be given to you as well (Luke 12:31).

If you can gift your children with an understanding of this key biblical principle, you will be rearing children who not only know about God, but who also know Him intimately!

Getting There

Okay, let's grease the God cogs. This week, sit down as a family and figure out several doors you would like to see opened to your family. Maybe the door is a new home or the money for ballet lessons or the salvation or healing of a friend. Everybody in the family gets to pick one outreach-oriented door and one door that is a desire of their heart. This could be anything from a new doll for your toddler to a trip to the Bahamas for the entire family. Keep track of these things in your journal.

For seven days, you are going to seek God as a family on these things. Gather your family and let them know that you are going on a seeking adventure. Get the list and lay it in the middle of your family circle. Then forget about the list while you all focus on Jesus. You can put some worship music on or just talk together about how good Jesus is. The key is to set your eyes on Him and not the things you are seeking.

Next, you will want to pray that the Holy Spirit will speak to your hearts. Spend a few minutes in silence and then interview everyone as to what tugged on his or her heart. Keep a journal of what everyone thinks that he or she heard.

Finish by reading a portion of God's Word from whatever daily reading plan you follow. Feel free to use an age-appropriate Bible for the sake of younger children. If anything you read from God's Word lines up with what you think you heard in your listening time, write it down to be tested. Be particularly aware of times when you are all hearing the same thing and then it gets reaffirmed through Scripture. Finish by praying that God would lead you into His will for these areas.

CHAPTER

11

The Word-based Decision

*Good and evil both increase at compound interest. That is why the little
decisions you and I make every day are of such infinite importance.*

C. S. LEWIS

Lil' Swimmer Puppy had become an obsession. Lily had to have it.
It was Saturday morning and the cartoons were flowing. Saturday
mornings are different from other mornings. On Saturdays we let
the girls watch a few coveted shows on the national networks. Unlike PBS, network shows come with commercials full of "stuff."

If you are like us, you don't watch many commercials these
days. Technology has made them an option rather than a requirement. This morning, the Lil' Swimmer Puppy commercial was taking up quite a bit of airtime.

If you aren't familiar with Lil' Swimmer Puppy,[1] he is a robotic
plastic dog with kicking legs who is supposed to swim around in
the bathtub or pool making merry. That's about all he does.

Like most kids, Lily has her own private stash of cash. It is broken up into three parts: giving, savings and spending. Upon a thor-
ough count, Lily determined that she was quite a few bucks short
for the puppy to end all puppies to become a reality.

Luckily for her it was a workday. With the option to contract
out for extra cash, Lily could bridge this gap. Contract labor at our
home is not the easy jobs like making your bed and taking out trash.
It is yard work, the kind of work you do with shovels and hoes.

Three hours later, Lily, with my assistance in the yard, had earned the cash to buy the aquatic pup. From that point on, Lily went into pester mode. I am sure you know this offensive child tactic. Before long I had promised to take her to the local mercantile to purchase Lil' Swimmer Puppy.

When we left, I noticed that her savings jar and tithe jar were empty. I asked her about this; she said that she was only going to do this once and that she always tithes and saves and wanted to make this one exception.

Since we find it counterproductive to force our children to tithe, I let her make this decision. As parents, Karie and I are trying to shape willing hearts, not create right behavior based on "shoulds." The Scripture is clear that if what you do is not done with the right attitude it loses its Kingdom value.

Each man should give what he has decided in his heart to give, not reluctantly or under compulsion, for God loves a cheerful giver (2 Cor. 9:7).

Before we left to get the toy, I opened the Word of God with Lily and talked about why we give to God. I did everything in my power to make sure there was no guilt involved, but I wanted her to understand some of the scriptural reasons. I also asked if she wanted to process this decision with one of her grandmas before she left. Nannas Ginny and Pat are always a comfort and a voice of wisdom in these situations. Wise counsel is a biblical step in decision-making.

As you can imagine, Lily wanted nothing to do with her two nannas on this occasion. To make a long story short, the $30 swimming puppy ended up being a bust. By the end of the day he was full of water and had lost his luster. Lily wanted to take him back and was frustrated that her coffers were empty.

While this story is pretty tame in the realm of employing godly wisdom, it creates a baseline of walking in the Spirit for the time when Lil' Swimmer Puppy turns into a decision about Mr. Right or whether or not to get into the car of a kid who has been drinking.

Like a junction on the 395 Highway to Mammoth, every decision we make is a crossroads. Each good or bad decision builds upon each other to create a life that is either lived in the Spirit or in the flesh, a life of blessing or futility.

The most powerful quote I have ever read on this is one by C. S. Lewis from *Mere Christianity*:

> Good and evil both increase at compound interest. That is why the little decisions you and I make every day are of such infinite importance. The smallest good act today is the capture of a strategic point from which, a few months later, you may be able to go on to victories you never dreamed of. An apparently trivial indulgence in lust or anger today is the loss of a ridge or railway line or bridgehead from which the enemy may launch an attack otherwise impossible.[2]

I'm not sure that we can be too vigilant in our pursuit of teaching godly decision-making to our children. Godly decisions are hewn in the trenches of success and failure. Parents who are trying to craft a sustainable faith in their children have allowed them to make decisions and either suffer or be blessed by the consequences.

I understand why we don't do this. As parents, we find it hard to let our children fail. We don't want our children to experience pain. But, as C. S. Lewis says, "God whispers to us in our pleasures, speaks in our conscience, but shouts in our pains; it is His megaphone to rouse a deaf world."[3] Lily learned a little more about stewardship when Lil' Swimmer Puppy sank to the bottom of the tub than she would have if I had just bought the toy for her. She was upset and cried that she had wasted her money, and she wanted it back.

I recently heard a preacher challenge his listeners to picture a child who got everything he or she ever wanted. The child was never told no, never allowed to experience pain. The preacher's well-taken point was that this creates monsters as opposed to children who walk in knowledge, wisdom and understanding.

How many important decisions do you allow your child to make? How good are you at letting your child fail? Do you give your children the opportunity to make decisions that have the ability to affect you? If you don't, I encourage you to do so with appropriate wisdom.

My friend Doug recently let his 15-year-old child decide the high school he wanted to go to. I know very few parents who would do this. One of the schools offered a better education and programs, the other a community of friends he had grown up with.

Decision-making is where the rubber meets the road in a full life in Christ. The more decisions you allow your child to make, with your proper direction and guidance, the greater the possibility of his or her sustainable faith beyond the family years.

It took all summer to make the decision, and, to be fair, it was one that Peyton had earned the right to make. Doug and Kristen have graduated him through a process of step-by-step decision-making. While Doug and Kristen had the final call, as is their scriptural charge, Peyton was still allowed a position of authority.

The thing I was impressed by was that Peyton's decision would affect the entire family. One school was further away and would put stress on the family routine. The other school had better sports programs, and with scholarships on the line, it was a big deal.

I cannot overstate how impressed I was by Doug and Kristen's willingness to pay a price to allow Peyton the opportunity to make important decisions. Whether your child is 2 or 15, you can do the same.

Encouraging Godly Decision-Making

If I had to pick an element of the Christian existence as most crucial, it would be decision-making. This is because decision-making employs all elements of walking in the Spirit. These are awareness, recognition, seeking, God's Word, prayer, obedience, faith, love, right action, and more.

Decision-making is where the rubber meets the road in a full life in Christ. The more decisions you allow your child to make, with your proper direction and guidance, the greater the possibility of his or her sustainable faith beyond the family years.

Reliance on the Word of God

The importance you put on the written word of God in your home is one barometer of the Spirit-led effectiveness of your family. Families with a reliance on the Word of God allow it to live for them every day.

There are many Scriptures that speak of the power and effectiveness of God's Word, but few rise off the page like Psalm 1. It is a road map to creating a family life full of God's providence and power.

> Blessed is the man who does not walk in the counsel of the wicked or stand in the way of sinners or sit in the seat of mockers. But his delight is in the law of the LORD, and on his law he meditates day and night. He is like a tree planted by streams of water, which yields its fruit in season and whose leaf does not wither. Whatever he does prospers (Ps. 1:1-3).

The promises in these verses are powerful, especially if you replace the word "man" with "the family." By taking the verse apart, you can visualize what your family would look like if this were true of you.

- **Planted by streams of water:** Your family will always have sustenance and provision.

- **Producing fruit in season:** Your family will have an abundance of fruitful living that is in line with God's timing for your lives. You will live on purpose!

- **You will not wither:** In tough, dry times, God will rain His blessing upon you.

- **Whatever you do will prosper:** Wow! This does not need more explanation.

The word "meditate" often conjures up images of monks sitting in silence. Another way to think about meditation is "focus." What are you focusing on? Think of the Word of God as the lens of a camera. The life you live is everything seen in the viewfinder. Things only become clear when you adjust the subject in the viewfinder through the focus of the lens. The same is true for life in the Word. Everything you see needs to be focused through the lens of Scripture.

Imagine what your family life would look like if you regularly brought the questions "How would God's Word view this situation?" or "Did the Bible live for us today?" into the conversations of your life? What if you asked these questions at least twice a day? How long do you think it would be until the Word of God shaped your family life in a deeper way? There is not a moment in your life when these questions can't be asked.

When things don't go your kid's way, these questions will bring the situation into perspective. When the car breaks down on the way to your family vacation, the Word of God will bring light. When your son or daughter loses a school friend to an accident or cancer, God's Word is there to bring light and clarity. Kingdom-building families apply what they know of God's character and nature from His Word into every circumstance of their life. Children who are taught to do this will see God shape and bless their lives. When God's Word becomes practical to you, blessing you and encouraging you when you are down, you will come to love it. There is a big difference between those who know God's Word and those who love, hunger and thirst for it.

Asking "Did the Bible live for us today?" with appropriate timing is an easy and powerful way to set up a pattern that allows your children to see life through the context of Scripture. Another positive is that when you don't know the answer to this question, you have just set a date to search the Word alongside your child for an answer. Go, once again, to the dig site!

Preeminent vs. Predominant

Like most areas of faith, your children will learn how to put life into the focus of Scripture from watching you. For this to happen, you may need to get your priorities straight. The Word of God will not only have to be predominant in your life, but preeminent. It's not hard for your children to spot the difference.

If you think about it, what you value as a priority can be easily seen. People who love golf share similarities with each other that make them quickly recognizable. People surround themselves with what they are interested in. They spend money on what they like. They commit their time to it. The same is true for parents who love and exalt the Word.

When things are predominant, they are common and familiar. Things that are preeminent are supreme. "Predominance" means "most common or conspicuous; main or prevalent"; while "preeminence" means "superior to or notable above all others; outstanding."[4] For example, when you get to heaven, angels will be a predominant component, but only Jesus will be preeminent.

I don't want to set up a system of rules for you to measure yourself and feel either proud or guilty. Carrying a giant Bible and memorizing verses will not make you a person of the Word. I have met many jerks who are full of God's Word, but they don't know how to put it into practice or how to live in love. I think I was actually one of those guys in college.

Today I would rather focus on the question "Does the Word of God live for your family every day?" If the Word lives for you every day, it means that at the end of each day you can see real instances where you made conscious decisions to walk a different way because of Scripture.

When these moments happen, tell your children. This was the pattern of Deuteronomy 6, using conversation to apply Scripture to real-life situations. The more you talk about it when you use

Scripture to direct your path, the deeper an impression you will leave on your children.

The only caveat is that your kids need to enter into the conversation and feel that they are adding something. What they don't need is a laundry list of how you are following God through His Word each day. That just gets boring and overbearing. Rather, ask them their opinion about what you observed. Challenge them to let you know when a verse of Scripture comes to mind during the day. Heck, bribe them with ice cream to do it. Whatever the motivation, get them processing life through God's lens and let them know that you are interested in them when they do!

Let Them Use the Word for Decision-making

Once or twice a week, I try to facilitate a time for each of the girls to seek God through His Word. For Lucy, our two-year-old, this means giving her the picture book Bible and asking her to find a good story about fish. The point is to get her actively looking into the Word for a purpose. I believe this will set in Lucy the basis of knowing that she can look to God's Word and find what she is looking for.

Starting when Lily was four or five, I began sending her to our home office with her Bible when she had an important decision to make. When she was younger, I asked her to draw a picture of anything that stuck out, anything that was interesting. When she was done, I worked with her to process any thoughts she came up with. We would apply her ideas to the situation. Sometimes we didn't get much, but other times it was clear what God was trying to say. Now, as an eight-year-old, I still challenge Lily to spend time with God, listening as she reads His Word. The difference is that she now goes into these times with a yellow pad and a pen instead of crayons and drawing paper.

The Word in a Tough Year

Last year was a rough school year for Lily. She had carried home a few disciplinary notes from the teacher and knew the next one meant a consequence. Around the middle of the year I arrived home to the news that Lily needed to talk to me. She was upset. She had brought another note home and was fearful of the coming consequence.

Something inside me told me that God wanted to go beyond what some of the normal consequences could foster in her heart. Instead of taking something away or grounding her, I told Lily that for the next three mornings when she woke up, I wanted her to take her Bible and a yellow pad and pen and spend 15 minutes reading God's Word. I figured that the point was behavioral change, not just getting through some discipline.

Something also told me that God's Word was the solution. I told her to keep track of any type of awareness, no matter how random. Just to be clear, this was an option for Lily. She was not forced to do this. If she chose not to, then we could revert to one of the standard models. Needless to say, she jumped at the time-with-God option.

The next morning, Lily beat me out of bed. When I woke up, I found her in the office spending time in the Word, her little pad scribbled with notes. I closed the door and let her continue.

Each night, Lily would process with me what she felt God might be saying. At the end of the third day, Lily told me that she felt the class did not challenge her, and when she was bored, she got in trouble. I fully agreed with her assessment. The next week, Karie and I asked the principal if Lily could be moved into a higher math and reading level.

Ms. Carter, our principal, thought this was a good idea. The next day, Lily was part of the more advanced groups. Lily did not bring another note home for the remaining five months of second grade. She finished the year strong, and in the process grew in her understanding of seeking God through the light of His written Word. In this case, discipline-as-usual was not the answer; the Word of God was.

Raise Your Expectations

A lot of the teaching I have heard about creating a family of the Word seems to be more about increasing the frequency kids see and hear the Word rather than giving them the opportunity to let it come alive. Yes, frequency in God's Word is crucial, but it can lead to rote repetition if children can't access it and walk in the light of God's revelation.

I am not sure why more parents don't expect their young children to be able to walk in the light of God's direction through His Word. The homework my daughter brings home from second grade expects and requires a much higher standard than most parents imagine their children attaining in this crucial spiritual realm. I would go as far as to say that many God-fearing, active parents are relaxed in this area of a child's spirituality.

> The homework my daughter brings home from second grade expects and requires a much higher standard than most parents imagine their children attaining in this crucial spiritual realm.

For the sake of comparison, think of the standard most parents have in the area of education. Recently in school, Lily was asked to read a story about Martin Luther King, Jr., to surmise the content and then logically process the lessons and personal takeaways. Next, the class was asked to write, in a logical pattern, what they learned and create a project together in the spirit of MLK. Is that not the intent and purpose of personal Bible study? It baffles me that I rarely see Christian children believed in and inspired to do this type of study of God's Word.

A Daily Invitation

Having a grasp of God's Word will allow your children to easily check if the promptings they are sensing are in line with the nature and character of God's Word. If they don't know God's Word, they are going to make poor decisions. This is why the book of Psalms uses the metaphor of the Word of God being like a lamp and a light for your path. You stub your toe a lot more in the dark than in the light.

Your word is a lamp to my feet and a light for my path (Ps.
119:105).

A great way to get your kids in the Word every day is by doing a
portion of your quiet time beside your child.

For a long time, I tried to get up earlier than my girls to have
some precious alone time. It seemed that the earlier I woke up the
earlier they did too. This was getting frustrating. Then one day God
prompted me to invite them into this time.

Now when they wake to find me reading the Word in the mornings, I invite them to get a blanket and cuddle up. Is this not what God
Himself invites us to do every morning with Him? I then begin to read
the Word to them, paraphrasing to bring clarity. After a few minutes
I hand them their picture Bibles and we all read and look separately.
When that time comes to an end after a few minutes, I get up and
make breakfast where we discuss what we read as we eat our pancakes.

I cannot overstate how much God has blessed this time. Not only
does it give us a reference point for the rest of the day for our discus-
sions of life in the Word, but I have also personally found great nour-
ishment for a day of pastoring God's flock. Oddly, before this, I saw
my girls' presence as a hindrance, but God has shown me another way.

I think that when we see our kids as an adversary to our times alone
with God, we are missing out on an important season in our life. God
understands and created this season for you. If you continue to try to
force what worked for you as a single, childless adult onto your life as
a parent, you are going to be out of season and you are going to be frus-
trated. Live in season. Sure, you need time carved out to be alone with
God, but the amount of time for that comes and goes with the seasons
of your life. I would also venture to assume that if most of us gave up
some of our coveted evening TV time after the kids go to bed, there
would be plenty of time to sit in quiet with Jesus.

If you have the ability to bring your kids into your personal quiet
time, I encourage you to do so. Jesus did this often with His disciples.
The garden of Gethsemane is probably the greatest example we know of.

This model will deeply impact the entirety of your life. The atmo-
sphere you create in your home each morning will profoundly affect

your child. If your morning is frantic and frenetic, it will become a template for the entire day. Instead, make that template a day that begins in God's Word.

God's Word Is Life

God often uses a verse from my morning readings throughout the day, but it is the backlog of regular readings that I usually refer to.

The importance of this was highlighted to me recently in Britt Merrick's book *Big God* in a passage about the day that he and his wife found out their five-year-old daughter, Daisy Love, had stage-four cancer.

> Precepts and passages came quickly. And we didn't have to open the Bible. We didn't need someone to come along and quote Scripture to us. It was just there, because we had done one simple thing in life: we had committed to reading our Bibles.[5]

On the day that Britt and Kate got this news, they were faced with many invitations. I am sure the devil was right there along with the world and the voice of the flesh to give their opinions. Thankfully, the Merricks had years of experience in applying Scripture to the story of their life. In the big and the small of life, God's Word had become part of their journey. For Britt and his family, life is lived in God's Word and God's Word is life. There is no separation.

As I look back at some of the biggest mistakes of my teen years, I can see that, while I knew the Word, it had never really penetrated my life to where I used it in daily situations. I knew its message, but not its heart. As I think about my girls' future, I want to make sure they do not end up with the same dilemma.

The Bible Is Not a Book of Magic

Some people try to use God's Word as a divining rod. For example, let's say that you and your son are trying to decide which teacher they should request for the following year. Let's also say that one of the teacher's names is Ms. Sharon. On the first day of seeking the Lord, you and your son come across this gem:

I am a rose of Sharon, a lily of the valleys (Song of Sol. 2:1).

That might seem ridiculous to many of you, but I know so many people who make decisions with this type of biblical revelation. While I don't want to limit the way God can speak to us, I do want to suggest that this is risky biblical interpretation. I call this fortune cookie Christianity. The person who does this is looking for a verse that seems to confirm something he is seeking God for, without taking in the whole counsel of God's Word, and immediately deciding that this is a "God-incidence." This is no different than thrusting a finger into the Bible and pulling out the first verse you touch as marching orders for the day.

I am not saying that God does not direct us occasionally with Scriptures that relate to our circumstances, but I think we are much closer to the Bible's directional intent when we use God's Word to guide us into value-driven decisions rather than pinpoint answers.

Let's look again at Ms. Sharon's class. Instead of looking for direct answers like the word "Sharon" popping up in the Bible, use the Scriptures to help your child check his heart and intent.

Let's assume that Ms. Sharon is the highest-rated teacher. Okay, that is a great reason to want to be in her class. Let's also say that your son has developed a special relationship with two special-needs children who will not be placed in that class. In our school, one or two special-needs children are mainstreamed into each class. Maybe your son is the only one who cares for these two boys and has become a major blessing in their lives. He makes sure they don't get picked on, that they do get to play in the handball game, and so on.

Now here is the tough question: Would you and your child sacrifice a possibly better education for the sake of your son's ability to shepherd and minister to these two special-needs boys, believing that it is God's purpose that your son's education will be blessed?

With this type of approach, instead of seeing verses about "Sharon" jump off the page, you will instead be teaching your children to make decisions with their heart based on the small inner voice and on the very character of God.

Be Willing to Make Godly Wrong Decisions

The Bible is clear that God wants a contrite heart first and accurate decision-making second. I see no biblical command that says we can't step out with a pure heart and bold faith and get it completely wrong. As a matter of fact, the Scriptures tell us that even if we get it wrong, God will make it right.

> And we know that in all things God works for the good of those who love him, who have been called according to his purpose (Rom. 8:28).

I firmly believe that you could arrive in heaven after living a life of trying to discern the right decisions, but getting them all wrong, and still hear God say, "Well done, good and faithful servant." God is looking at the intent of the heart, not perfect decision-making. Proverbs 16 assures us that we will never get it right anyway, but we can trust that God will:

> To man belong the plans of the heart, but from the LORD comes the reply of the tongue. All a man's ways seem innocent to him, but motives are weighed by the LORD. Commit to the LORD whatever you do, and your plans will succeed. The LORD works out everything for his own ends—even the wicked for a day of disaster (Prov. 16:1-4).

I find this passage so comforting and full of grace. I don't have to teach my kids to find that pinpoint area in the perfect center of God's will and purpose for a given situation. Rather, we encourage our girls to understand the message of the Bible as a whole and to make decisions based on that heart—the heart of love.

Letting your kids know that God can and will bless every decision they make if done with a contrite and humble heart will help them to become less stuck in their decision-making. It will also help them use God's Word to focus on the type of person they are called to be and how to align their hearts with the heart of God rather than getting stuck in trying to find God's one perfect plan.

Using God's Word for the direction of our lives is not about right answers, but about a right heart no matter what you or they decide! Oddly, Proverbs 16:1-3 tells us that we never will know the true motive of any decision we make:

> To man belong the plans of the heart, but from the LORD comes the reply of the tongue. All a man's ways seem innocent to him, but motives are weighed by the LORD. Commit to the LORD whatever you do, and your plans will succeed.

The reassuring aspect of this Scripture is that God promises to direct our step toward His perfect conclusion. Godly decision-making is not about the right decision but about making a decision with the right heart.

Here's a good rule of thumb: Have your children apply the following Scriptures from 1 Corinthians 13 to every decision they make, and they will never go wrong!

> If I speak in the tongues of men and of angels, but have not love, I am only a resounding gong or a clanging cymbal. If I have the gift of prophecy and can fathom all mysteries and all knowledge, and if I have a faith that can move mountains, but have not love, I am nothing. If I give all I possess to the poor and surrender my body to the flames, but have not love, I gain nothing.
>
> Love is patient, love is kind. It does not envy, it does not boast, it is not proud. It is not rude, it is not self-seeking, it is not easily angered, it keeps no record of wrongs. Love does not delight in evil but rejoices with the truth. It always protects, always trusts, always hopes, always perseveres.
>
> Love never fails. But where there are prophecies, they will cease; where there are tongues, they will be stilled;

where there is knowledge, it will pass away. For we know in part and we prophesy in part, but when perfection comes, the imperfect disappears. When I was a child, I talked like a child, I thought like a child, I reasoned like a child. When I became a man, I put childish ways behind me. Now we see but a poor reflection as in a mirror; then we shall see face to face. Now I know in part; then I shall know fully, even as I am fully known (vv. 1-12).

A decision made in love is eternal and never misses its mark. Love never fails. Teach your kids to decide with the heart of love.

Getting There

Make God's Word preeminent today.

Invite your kids into your times with God. Don't force this, but if they interrupt you, invite them in. God is never inconvenienced by you, so model the same to your children.

Invest financially in some Bible-based curriculum to use in your car with the kids. There is plenty out there.

Put an open Bible in every major living area of your home (kitchen, family room, dining room). Make sure some Bibles are age appropriate to your kids. Find a two-year-read-through-the-Bible program online and turn the pages every day. There is something special about having the open Word of God displayed in your home.

Notes
1. This is not the real name of this product.
2. C. S. Lewis, *Mere Christianity* (San Francisco: HarperSanFrancisco, 2001).
3. C. S. Lewis, *The Problem of Pain* (San Francisco: HarperSanFrancisco, 2001).
4. *The American Heritage Dictionary of the English Language,* fourth edition (New York: Houghton Mifflin Company, 2000), s.v. "predominance" and "preeminence."
5. Britt Merrick, *Big God* (Ventura, CA: Regal, 2010).

The Conversation of Prayer

*To be a Christian without prayer is no more possible than
to be alive without breathing.*
MARTIN LUTHER KING JR.

Recently, our friend Lauren was cleaning her house while her two-year-old, Annabelle, was playing in her room. Things were getting a little too quiet, so Lauren decided to check on her daughter. When she did, she was blown away. There was Annabelle praying over her stuffed animals and thanking God for her house. Annabelle was praying when her mom was not looking!

Outside of a movement of the Holy Spirit in Annabelle's life, there is only one reason why Annabelle was caught praying when no one was looking. Annabelle comes from a family that prays and has made prayer a part of the conversation of their life.

Here's an excerpt from Lauren's email:

I caught Annabelle praying by herself a couple of weeks ago. Thanking Jesus for her stuffed animals and her house. Yesterday she looked at the sky when we were sitting at the park and said, "I know I'm blessed." What?! So, thanks. I'm sure what you've shared with me is playing a part.

The Conversation of Prayer

While prayer is difficult for everyone, it becomes easier if we begin to make it part of the conversation of our life. Think about it this way. Your life is a conversation. Some parts of the conversation only come up a few times. Other topics, like your job and school are referred to on a regular basis. These conversations are the conversation of your life and, in the end, will tell the story of your life in the same way that a screenplay tells the story of the movie it represents.

> While prayer is difficult for everyone,
> it becomes easier if we begin to make it
> part of the conversation of our life.

You have the ability to enrich the conversation and story of your life by inserting prayer on a regular basis. When we add prayer into our life's conversation, it brings meaning and power and deepens our connection with the Author of our story.

The place to start is once again to recognize all of the prayer opportunities that surround you and your children. Every time you hear a siren, you have been given an opportunity to pray. Each time you pass a homeless person on the street, you have been given an opportunity to pray. When you wake, prayer awaits you. When you start any journey in the car, a prayer of safety is presented to you. When your kids start their homework, another prayer for understanding is at your doorstep. You see, prayer is life, and your life is a prayer.

> Prayer is life, and your life is a prayer.

Micro-prayer

"Micro-prayers" are the prayers that decompartmentalize your spirituality; they turn your life into a prayer. In Ephesians 6:18, Paul talks about this type of prayer.

And pray in the Spirit on all occasions with all kinds of prayers and requests. With this in mind, be alert and always keep on praying for all the saints.

What Paul is saying is, don't miss prayer in the routines of your life. Be alert, and when you become aware of an opportunity, PRAY!

What would life look like if you began to pray like this with your children? Let's say you began by praying five micro-prayers a day. When your child tells you that he has a sore throat, you will pray a quick prayer of healing. When she tells you about a friend from school whose parents are separating, you will pray for their family. When you drop your kids off at the bus stop, you will pray a micro-prayer of blessing over them. Soon you will be praying more than you have ever prayed in your life.

Before you know it, your kids will begin to be the ones to initiate the prayers. Maybe you have already experienced this at mealtime. I know that if we forget to pray over a meal, our two-year-old, Lucy, will remind us that we need to pray. Why does this happen? It happens because we, like you, have conditioned our children to pray at certain times.

Let prayer break the boundaries of your child's bedroom and family's dinner table. In other words, don't let these areas be the only place your children are taught to pray. In this way you will be doing what the Bible calls praying without ceasing. At the same time you will be teaching your kids that prayer is not just for quiet times and church but is to be released into the whole story of your life.

Pray continually [without ceasing] (1 Thess. 5:17).

This type of prayer is easily accessible to busy moms and has the power to impress a legacy of prayer on your children. Rather than waiting for life to offer up perfect moments for prayer, take the bull by the horns and create them yourself.

I heard a woman say once, "Little prayer will bring little answers. Big prayer will bring big answers." What she meant by this was that the more you pray, the more answered prayer you will experience. Only prayers that are prayed will get a chance to be answered.

Prayer Is Always the Answer

My mother is a woman of prayer. She recently gave me a book on praying the Scriptures. On the inside cover, she wrote, "Prayer is always the answer." The moment I read it, something inside me changed. God added to my understanding and changed the way I see prayer and have lived since.

The more I thought about it, the more I realized there is not a situation in life, whether difficult or glorious, where prayer cannot be applied.

When your child is not assigned to the teacher of your choice, prayer is the answer. When a decision needs to be made between ballet and soccer, prayer is the answer. When your son is faced with a difficult relationship or a bully, prayer is the answer. As a matter of fact, every twist in the story of your life has its solution in prayer.

I want to challenge you to make this phrase, "Prayer is the answer," and more importantly, the prayers that follow a part of your life's conversation. The more you sow into this phrase and the prayers that follow, the more you will begin to trust in God and prayer as a means to finding the path of your family's life.

Here is how you do it. The next time there is a dilemma of any kind that you don't currently have the solution to, remind everyone that God answers prayer and that prayer is the answer.

There is definitely an art to this, and there are times when it is better to let everyone find some emotional balance in the family before you hit them with your new patented "Prayer is the answer" mantra. In the same way that "location, location, location" is the key to launching a restaurant, "timing, timing, timing" is the key to landing faith-building prayers.

Once you feel that the timing is right, just say, "Hey, guys, we believe that God answers prayer, right? Well, maybe prayer is the answer to this as well. Let's shoot up a quick prayer about it."

Praying like this takes so much of the mystery out of prayer and shrinks it down a bit. It makes it more accessible. It makes prayer a real and viable part of your life and disciples your children to seek God in prayer in all the situations of their life.

If children feel that prayer is so big that they have to pull out a sacramental robe or put the ephod of King David on, they will never experience it for themselves. Rather, prayer will be a distant art used only by the most godly pastors and religious missionary people, in the most distant of foreign lands.

One day when they are in college and hoping to get that scholarship, they will remember that Mom or Dad always told them, "Prayer is always the answer." And someday when they have children of their own, they will pass this legacy of prayer down to their children saying, "Grandma always said that prayer is the answer. So let's pray!"

Prayers for Blue Bear

We recently saw the use of this phrase come to life with Lucy, our two-year-old. It was bedtime, and we could not find the coveted "Blue Bear." In our home, sleep does not happen unless Blue Bear finds his way through the travails of a toddler's day and back to Lucy's bed. On this night, Blue Bear was nowhere to be found. As we were looking, Lucy stopped crying during the search and started to pray, "Jesus, help me find my Blue Bear!" Moments later, Blue Bear was found and we were all able to get some sleep.

What Karie and I were most pleased about was that Lucy felt that praying to Jesus was the solution to her dilemma. This is because we have heeded my mother's wisdom that prayer is always the answer.

Prayer Is About Relationship

This was not the first time that we had prayed for Blue Bear. Since Blue Bear is a family member, we pray for him all of the time. When I was first cutting my teeth as the parent of a toddler, with

Lily, I was a little apprehensive to teach her to pray real prayers over inanimate objects.

God has shown me that prayer is about relationship. God does not need us to pray, rather He allows us to pray because He wants us to be in relationship with Him. God meets us all where we are. For toddlers like Lucy, the separation between what is real and what is fiction is a thin line. To her, Blue Bear is real and has real problems that she cares about. Lucy figures that if God is good for what ails her, then He is good for what ails Blue Bear. Thus, we have prayed for Blue Bear when he is sad and when he is hurt. Lucy has even led him to Jesus, assuring us that Jesus is in his heart.

At some point in her normal development, Lucy will discover that Blue Bear is not real, at least no more real then the Velveteen Rabbit. But the lessons of compassion and faith that God has taught Lucy through Blue Bear are most definitely real and will last for eternity.

They Won't Believe It If You Don't

Do you believe that prayer is the answer? If you don't, it will be very difficult to impress it upon your kids. You will know that prayer is the answer when you stop trying to control everything in your own power—when you stop trying to manipulate. You will know that prayer has become the answer whenever you are faced with a turn in the road and your mind moves toward prayer before fleshly solutions. You will know that prayer has become your answer when you lose your keys and believe that praying about it is the place to start looking. You will know that prayer has become your answer when your kids begin to remind you to pray, recalling your own words that prayer is always the answer.

Don't Force It

While Karie and I do ask for respect during times of family prayer, we don't force our kids to pray. And we try never to show any form of disappointment when they don't want to join into the family prayers. Sure, we want them to pray, and we do our best to teach them how to pray, but our hope is that they will see the value of prayer and pray on their own.

One thing we do try to do is to give our girls the opportunity to pray. Like you and me, our children will have times of spiritual dryness, times when they will want to assert spiritual independence. These are the seasons when they don't want to pray and seem bored during any spiritual exercise.

First of all, let me reiterate that prayer is always the answer. While these times can be concerning, they are normal. Your response to these times is crucial. When this happens, go to prayer. Pray that God will give you revelation to where your kids are spiritually. Pray that God will also lead you in walking your children through these times. Trust God.

When these or any tough times come, Karie and I have used a twofold approach that to this point has worked every time. The first thing we do is increase our time spent with that child. If we have to switch our entire schedule around, it will be done. Quality time with us is the answer to so many of our children's problems.

Since we are blessed to have access to a cabin in our local mountains, it usually means that Lily or Lucy is going to get at least a 24-hour retreat with either Mom or Dad. Everything else can wait. Ministry can most definitely wait. I will dig ditches before I will surrender my children to second place.

The next thing we do is put our children's faith in their hands. When they don't want to pray with us, we try to create opportunities for them to pray when we are not looking. We give them more personal responsibility in the spiritual realm. Something like, "Hey, your uncle is having surgery this week and needs prayer. Would you remember to pray for him before you fall asleep tonight?"

Sometime later in the week, we will just ask her if she prayed for her uncle. If she says no, then fine, but you can be sure that another prayer challenge is right around the corner. The point is that rather than making them perform spiritual rituals, we want them to know that we trust them and have faith in their personal walk with Christ. To this point we have found that Lily will pray when challenged in this way. Is this not a better model than bowed heads and closed eyes with no participation of the heart?

Nothing will build your child's prayer life faster than knowing that you truly value not only their prayers, but also their ability to hear from God.

When we recently toyed with the idea of selling our home, we let Lily be part of that decision. We encouraged her to pray and ask God to speak to her. We told her to listen to the quiet voice in her heart and relate to us what she heard the next day.

Guess what? The next day Lily let us know that she felt God did not want us to move. Whether this was God or Lily's desire to stay put is not as important to us as the fact that she went to God for an answer.

As the spiritual lead of our home, I want you to know that I often take my children's spiritual voice into my decision-making process. I am surprised at how many parents never ask their kids for advice or godly counsel in important family matters.[1]

If this seems like a stretch for you, just think about how big of a stretch it is for God to hear and consider your prayers. I can assure you that the gap between your child's spiritual wisdom and maturity is smaller than yours is to God's. When Abraham prayed to God for Sodom, asking God, "What if the number of the righteous [in the city] is five less than fifty? Will you destroy the whole city because of five people?" God replied, "If I find forty-five there, I will not destroy it" (Gen. 18:28). Later, Moses had a similar interaction with God:

> But Moses sought the favor of the LORD his God. "O LORD," he said, "why should your anger burn against your people, whom you brought out of Egypt with great power and a mighty hand? Why should the Egyptians say, 'It was with evil intent that he brought them out, to kill them in the mountains and to wipe them off the face of the earth'? Turn from your fierce anger; relent and do not bring disaster on your people. Remember your servants Abraham, Isaac and Israel, to whom you swore by your own self:

'I will make your descendants as numerous as the stars in the sky and I will give your descendants all this land I promised them, and it will be their inheritance forever.'" *Then the LORD relented and did not bring on his people the disaster he had threatened* (Exod. 32:11-14, emphasis added).

By not involving your children in the spiritual guidance of your home, you are telling them their spiritual voice has no value. You are unknowingly communicating that spiritual knowledge and guidance from God is something you get when you grow up. In this way, you are setting up an obstacle they will have to climb once they reach the imagined barrier you have helped create. Then they will have to decide to accept the faith you have given them and learn to hear and value their own spiritual voice. Many young people never clear this hurdle, and they leave the church altogether. As I mentioned in chapter 2, this number currently stands at 60 percent of all children who are raised in the church.

Kids who have been allowed to be a prayerful participant in their family's spiritual journey are those who have been told their voice matters. They are children who will eventually give insights from God that you have not asked for. They are the children who have been given an opportunity to seek God in prayer and experience the effects of that seeking. They are children who will pray when you are not looking.

Getting There

This week, try to pray with your children five times a day (in addition to dinner and bedtime). At any point in the day that seems appropriate, stop and pray about a situation that arises. You don't even have to close your eyes. These prayers can happen almost anywhere.

Make a decision this week to live as if prayer is always the answer. Ask God to reveal to you times that He is inviting you into prayer when this would not normally be your first inclination.

Make a note card this week to tape to the ceiling above your kids' beds that says "Prayer Is Always the Answer!"

Ask your son or daughter to pray about an important issue in regard to family life. Ask later in the week if God gave him or her any good ideas. Rather than saying, "Did God speak to you?" just say, "Did God give you any good ideas?" Children are more likely to enter into this type of question.

Give your kids great encouragement whenever they share with you what they felt God told them, even if they say something that might be contrary to Scripture. Trust me, you and I have gotten it wrong lots of times. Instead say, "Thank you so much for sharing that with me. Let me think about this and get back to you." This way they will feel valued. Contradicting them in the moment might teach them to share less. If they know you have prayed about what they said before you respond, they will begin to value their spiritual voice. Maybe even God will show you something you have never thought about before.

Ask your kids to pray when you are not with them. At night, let them know that bedtime prayers are just the start of their nightly prayer times. Encourage them to talk to God after you leave the room. I can't take credit for this challenge. I wrote it down after Lily told me that she likes to pray best in bed after bedtime prayers and stories. Without realizing it, we had been setting up a barrier to her prayers. We had unconsciously created a model that said prayer time was over when we left the room. Thankfully, Lily was not willing to let the prayers end once we finished praying with her.

On my bed I remember you; I think of you through the watches of the night (Ps. 63:6).

Note

1. Note that godly wisdom is necessary in this pursuit. Obviously, some decisions are not appropriate to allow children to process.

Conclusion

Pray to Him
by Lily Stadtmiller

If you love the Lord, pray to Him. My aunt and uncle were going to have a baby, but they were having problems. Lucy, my sister, always prayed for them. She said, "Jesus, I pray for Albie and Antje and baby in tummy." The baby came out safely. Love the Lord.

During the final edit of this manuscript, I received a phone call from a friend and teacher on campus at Kelly Elementary while a recent school shooting was in progress. Kelly is next to our district, and many of Lily's friends from church were on the playground when the shooter began his rampage. Praise God for some construction workers, one with whom I went to high school, who raced to the scene before any children were killed and subdued the man. Thanks to their daring courage, only two second-graders were grazed with bullets in their arms from the man's weapon.

The aftermath of this event showed me how fear can sweep into a community. Granted, fear is one of my strongholds, so it has tried its best to get a grip on my heart as well.

For the last four years, God has had me praying against an event of this sort in our district. Two days prior to the shooting, on a run, God prompted me to pray again as I passed our daughter's school.

I found out later that on the morning of the shooting, our local Mom's in Touch groups had prayer-walked Kelly Elementary. My pastor, Mark Foreman, said to me on the following Sunday, "Do you know the difference between the six inches that separate a bullet hitting a child's arm instead of his or her heart? Prayer."

Love God, believe in your kid's spiritual potential, and fear not!

Our warmest hearts regard,
Adam, Karie, Lily and Lucy

About the Authors

Adam and Karie Stadtmiller have been in ministry
together for more than 15 years, serving in various organizations
around the world. They currently minister at North Coast Calvary
Chapel in Carlsbad, California, where Adam oversees the
30-something ministry. Together, they have two daughters,
Lily Kate (8) and Lucy Joy (3).

If you would like to book Adam and Karie for a
conference or event, please contact them at
bookings@adamstadtmiller.com

Find Adam on Facebook by searching Adam Stadtmiller,
or follow him on Twitter by doing the same.

Adam also writes a weekly blog that you can find at
adamstadtmiller.com

To download small-group discussion
guides, watch chapter video introductions,
and discuss the concepts of this book, go to
www.giveyourkidsthekeys.com